# A
# Jewish Family
# in Britain

# A
# Jewish Family in Britain

## Vida Barnett

Department of
Religious Studies,
City of Liverpool College of Higher Education

**Religious and Moral Education Press**
*An Imprint of Arnold-Wheaton*

The Religious and Moral Education Press
*An Imprint of Arnold-Wheaton*
Hennock Road, Exeter EX2 8RP

Pergamon Press Ltd
Headington Hill Hall, Oxford OX3 0BW

Pergamon Press Inc.
Maxwell House, Fairview Park, Elmsford, New York 10523

Pergamon Press Canada Ltd
Suite 104, 150 Consumers Road, Willowdale, Ontario M2J 1P9

Pergamon Press (Australia) Pty Ltd
P.O. Box 544, Potts Point, N.S.W. 2011

Pergamon Press GmbH
Hammerweg 6, D-6242 Kronberg, Federal Republic of Germany

First published 1983
Reprinted 1984

Printed in Great Britain by A. Wheaton & Co. Ltd, Exeter

ISBN 0 08-027888-4 non net
ISBN 0 08-027889-2 net

# Contents

FOREWORD 1

1 ROSH HASHANAH: A HAPPY NEW YEAR 3

2 YOM KIPPUR: THE DAY OF ATONEMENT
AND FORGIVENESS 10

3 TO HATE – OR TO FORGIVE 16

4 SUCCOTH: THE FESTIVAL OF
TABERNACLES 20

5 SIMCHAT TORAH: REJOICING IN THE LAW 27

6 MIRIAM CELEBRATES HER BIRTHDAY 32

7 SHABBAT: THE SABBATH 38

8 CHANUKAH: THE FESTIVAL OF
DEDICATION 46

9 A WEDDING IN THE FAMILY 53

10 PURIM: A FESTIVAL OF HOPE 58

11 PASSOVER: A FESTIVAL OF FREEDOM 64

12 A DEATH IN THE FAMILY 72

13 SHAVUOT: THE FESTIVAL OF PENTECOST 77

14 DAVID CELEBRATES HIS BAR-MITZVAH 86

RESOURCES/USEFUL ADDRESSES 91

GLOSSARY 93

## ACKNOWLEDGEMENTS

Photographs are reproduced by kind permission of the following:

BBC Hulton Picture Library
The Council of Christians and Jews
Peter Fisher
Sidney Harris
Jewish Chronicle
Jewish Education Bureau
The Jewish Museum
Jewish Programme Materials Project
Juliette John
John Rifkin
The Warburg Institute
Peter Woodward

Cover photograph by kind permission of the Council of Christians and Jews.

The illustration of the tallith on p. 11 previously appeared in the *Illustrated Dictionary of World Religions* (R.M.E.P.).

*For Bert*
*Thank you for three wonderful and precious years*

# Foreword

This is a story about an imaginary Orthodox Jewish family living in Britain. We share some of their experiences during the year preceding the bar-mitzvah of the older son, David. David's sister, Miriam, is fourteen, and they both go to nearby comprehensive schools. The younger brother, Paul, attends the local Jewish primary school. The children live with their parents and their grandmother.

It might be expected that if there was a Jewish primary school in the area, then there would be a Jewish secondary school also, and the older children would go there. But I have deliberately brought in both Jewish and non-Jewish schools so that readers may glimpse the kind of life Jewish children might lead, wherever they are educated. We may also see how Jewish class-mates can contribute to the personal and religious development of pupils in a State school, and this may lead teachers to seek opportunities for enrichment in their own class-rooms.

The multi-faith curriculum is not followed merely in order that we may learn *about* a number of religious communities. We *share* with people of different faiths their quest for answers to ultimate questions, for example those related to suffering, death, forgiveness and celebration. In dialogue we grow as people and in the enrichment of our experience we learn to make meaningful decisions. I hope that this book will let us share vicariously in Jewish family life, so that we may understand in some measure what it means to be a Jew.

1

Of course, the single-family approach pushes one headfirst into the pit of generalization. All Jewish families do not act and think in precisely this way. Readers must constantly bear this in mind. In all religious traditions there are different shades of belief and practice – though the central core of a faith remains the same for all. Thus we will not only find differences between the ultra-Orthodox Jews of Gateshead and Stamford Hill, and the Orthodox and Reform communities throughout the country, but we will also find small differences between members of each individual community. All I can say in mitigation of this book is that everything it describes and mirrors has either been shared by myself or has been told to me by Jewish friends and colleagues – and I thank them for all their help.

Many Religious Education teachers feel they cannot – or should not – attempt to "get inside" a faith to which they are not committed. I believe they should try to do so – and this book is an attempt to show that in some degree it is possible.

My special thanks must go to Moshe Davis, Executive Director of the Office of the Chief Rabbi in London. His generous, thoughtful, and speedy advice on reading the manuscript was invaluable. And without the help of Peter Woodward, who advised from the beginning and gave constant help in the practical tasks necessary before a book is put into print, there would have been no *A Jewish Family in Britain*. They share any success the book may have – but the faults are all mine.

# 1
# Rosh Hashanah:
# A Happy New Year

Paul threw his cap and satchel on to a chair and rushed into the kitchen, where his mother and grandmother were preparing the evening meal.

"Look at the New Year card I've made!" he cried. On the front he'd painted a **rabbi** wearing a prayer shawl and blowing a curved bone trumpet, a **shofar**, made from a ram's horn. In the background was the Western Wall in Jerusalem, all that remains today of the wall surrounding the old Jewish **Temple**.

*Many Jews visit the Western Wall in Jerusalem at festival times.*

3

He seized the pile of New Year cards which his mother had been addressing.

"We've got a large map of the world on our class-room wall. We're going to put flags in all the places where our friends live."

His mother laughed. "You'll need a lot of flags. Jews live in so many countries."

Paul glanced quickly through the envelopes. "Here's a card for Uncle Anton in Warsaw, and one for Dad's friends in Budapest."

Gran smiled sadly. "Before 1939 we sent many cards to European countries, but now . . . ."

"How many countries can you find?" asked Mrs Singer.

"America, Chile, Israel, South Africa, Zambia, New Zealand – and England and Scotland, of course. That makes ten countries altogether! Did I tell you that our class has adopted a Jewish boy in Moscow? The Russians won't let him join the rest of his family in Israel, and he's very lonely. So we're all going to send him cards."

As he rushed upstairs to do his homework, he shouted over his shoulder, "Stephen's family aren't sending any cards this year. They're giving the money to Vietnamese refugees."

After tea, Paul's older brother, David, asked his father if he could look at some of his books. "On Wednesday afternoons we all work on our own projects. I want to write something about **Rosh Hashanah**."

"I'll help you," offered Mr Singer. They soon collected a mass of information, a mixture of history and legend.

"On this festival we remember many stories from the early days of our history," said Mr Singer. "But especially we remember that God created the world, and people, and the **Sabbath**. Some of the early teachers, or rabbis, believed that God forgave Adam his sins on Rosh Hashanah. And He promised Adam that, in the future, everyone who asked for forgiveness on this day would be forgiven."

"But why do we blow the shofar?"

4

"It is to remind us that the shofar was blown when God gave the **Torah**, the Law, to Moses in the wilderness. If we study the Law, we know if we have acted wrongly, and so we know when we need forgiveness. When we ask for forgiveness during this festival, we blow the shofar in the synagogue."

*The prayers recited when the shofar is blown remind listeners that God is King of the Universe.*

5

David was looking at some pictures. "This shofar is very long and curly. I've never seen a ram with horns like this!"

"You can use the horn of any clean or **kosher** animal – except that of a cow. Remember the golden calf! But we often use a ram's horn to remind us that Abraham was willing to obey God, however difficult it might be."

"I remember," interrupted David. "He was even willing to sacrifice his son Isaac – but God sent a ram to be sacrificed in Isaac's place."

"The shofar is very hard to play; it takes a lot of practice."

"I know. The rabbi let us try at **bar-mitzvah** class. I couldn't make a sound!"


Miriam told her teacher she wouldn't be at school on Rosh Hashanah (New Year's Day), nor on **Yom Kippur**, the Day of Atonement. The rest of the class asked her to tell them something about the meaning of the festivals.

"At the beginning of the Jewish year we think about all the wrong things we've said and done during the previous twelve months," Miriam began. "We believe these hurt God as well as other people. On Rosh Hashanah we make a fresh start. The ten days between Rosh Hashanah and Yom Kippur are known as the ten days of penitence, when we repent of our sins. If we can, we try to make things up with the people we've hurt. We also pray to God and put a contribution in a collecting box in the synagogue. This money helps people who are old, or ill, or hungry, or homeless. Then, on Yom Kippur, the Day of Atonement and Forgiveness, we ask God to forgive us – and He does. Long ago a rabbi described it in picture language:

'On Yom Kippur God leaves His Throne of Judgement and sits on the Throne of Mercy. He is filled with compassion for us . . . He puts our names in the Book of Life.' That means He forgives us."

Her teacher laughed. "Now I know why you wrote on my New Year card, 'May you be inscribed and sealed in the Book of Life. A Happy and Prosperous New Year.'"

6

One of Miriam' friends looked thoughtful. "I suppose it was easier to ask people's forgiveness when everyone lived in small towns and villages."

"Yes, that's true," Miriam agreed. "Gran told me that long ago in Europe at this time of year a synagogue official called the **shamash** used to knock on doors and shutters late at night and early in the morning. The people would get up and go to the synagogue to study our sacred book, the Torah, to ask each other's forgiveness, and to say special prayers. These prayers were often very old, and many were written in times of persecution. We often say them today, because they remind us that God always helps us when we ask Him – though not always in the way we want!"

"Could you suggest a prayer we might use in Assembly next week?" the teacher asked.

"I like the one Gran taught me: 'May it be Thy will, O God, that we return to Thee in perfect penitence. Keep us free from hatred, bring us near to what Thou lovest, and deal mercifully with us. May it be Thy will, O God, that love and peace and brotherliness dwell among us.'"

The family arrived early at the synagogue. As always for this festival of Rosh Hashanah, the **Ark** and the **bimah** (platform) were covered with white cloths, and some of the officials were wearing white robes.

In answer to a question from Paul, Mr Singer said, "White represents joy. Today we are joyful because we know God forgives us."

The service began. Members of the congregation were called up to read from the sacred scrolls. One reading told of Abraham's willingness to give even his son, Isaac, to God.

In the sermon the rabbi said, "We often call this day the Day of Remembrance, because we remember our need for forgiveness. But a good Jew should ask God to forgive him every day."

The congregation recited Psalm 27: "The Lord is my light and my salvation", and said many prayers. David had learnt some of them at bar-mitzvah class. He especially liked the one which said, "God will say unto Israel, even to all humanity, 'My children, I look upon you as if today, Rosh Hashanah, you have been made for Me anew.' " Later in the year, when the time came for his bar-mitzvah ceremony, David would be accepting responsibility before God for his own actions, pledging himself to be a good Jew. That would be the beginning of a new life for him.

The shofar sounded. The strange, mournful notes echoed round the synagogue, as they would echo every day until the festival of Yom Kippur.

All the family enjoyed the special Rosh Hashanah meal. They ate bread baked in various shapes. There were ladders (a symbol of prayers rising to God), birds (because God had mercy even on the birds), and crowns (because God, the Creator, is King of the World). They dipped their first piece of bread in honey, saying, "May God give me a sweet and happy New Year". For dessert there were apples, covered in honey. Paul ate three!

David asked his father about some pictures he had found while preparing for his project. They showed Jews praying by rivers and on the sea-shore, throwing crumbs on to the water. "We call this **Tashlich**, which means 'cast away'," explained Mr Singer. "The crumbs represent bad actions and thoughts. The water represents cleansing. If possible, there should be fish in the water, reminding us that just as a fish can easily be caught in a net, so we can be easily caught by sin. Many Jews still follow this custom today."

Mrs Singer pushed back her chair. "Tell Paul a story, Gran, while the rest of us clear the table."

"In Poland there lived an old rabbi who loved God and his neighbours very much," the old lady began. "One morning he didn't arrive at the synagogue for the special prayers said during the week before Rosh Hashanah. The people had to start without him. On the second and third days he also missed the prayers. On the third night one of the congregation

*The ceremony of Tashlich is a relatively recent one, being only about 500 years old.*

hid in the rabbi's house. About midnight the old man got up and began to pray. He prayed for all Jews who were suffering in any way. Towards morning he dressed as a peasant and, carrying an axe and a rope, went out into the forest.

"The watcher followed. The rabbi chopped some logs and carried them back to a very poor cottage at the edge of the village. Inside lay a woman, very ill, shivering with cold. He made her a good fire, brought water from the well, and cooked a simple meal. All the time he repeated softly to himself the special Rosh Hashanah prayers. Very quietly the watcher crept away – and he told nobody in the village about what he had seen."

# 2
# Yom Kippur: The Day of Atonement and Forgiveness

Paul waited impatiently for Miriam and David to come home from school.

"Hurry up!" he said as they came in the front door. "Dad won't let me start tea without you, and I want time to have second helpings before we go to the synagogue. Even though I'm not fasting tomorrow, Dad says I mustn't eat or drink much all day, so I want a good meal this evening."

He turned to his brother. For the first time David was going to fast like his father and mother.

"David, why *do* we fast on Yom Kippur?"

"Well – because we have done wrong, we feel we should give up something we enjoy as a token that we are sorry and that we really deserve to be punished."

"Hurry up and get washed and changed," called their father.

Soon they were sitting round the table. Mr Singer blessed the food and then said, "Enjoy your meal. I know Yom Kippur is a solemn festival, but we can also be very happy, because we know God forgives us."

After helping to clear the table and wash up, the children stood waiting for their father's blessing.

"May it be the will of our Father in Heaven to plant in your hearts love of Him. May you wish to study the Torah and its commandments. May your lips speak the truth and your hands do good deeds. May you be inscribed and sealed for a long and happy life."

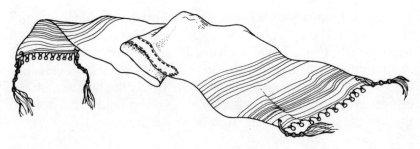

*Tallith*

Quietly they walked to the synagogue. David was surprised when his father put on his **tallith**, his prayer shawl. He'd forgotten that this was the one occasion in the year when a man wears his tallith at the evening service. They all shook hands with their relatives and friends, and said, "Forgive me if I've hurt you during the past year."

Many prayers were said, and then the rabbi and **cantor**, dressed in white, together with members of the congregation, opened the doors of the Ark and took out two of the Torah scrolls, wrapped up in white covers. They carried them quietly round the synagogue.

A beautiful and sad melody echoed round the building as the cantor began to recite the **Kol Nidre** prayer. Miriam listened carefully to the words which asked God's forgiveness for broken promises. Gran had told her how much this prayer had meant to persecuted Jews for many centuries. Sometimes, faced with torture and death, or simply with ridicule, they had failed to speak up for their faith. But God had understood their fears and forgiven them. It was very comforting! She remembered how once, when some girls had made fun of her because she wouldn't go with them to a disco on a Friday evening, she'd been tempted to make some silly excuse, instead of admitting that it was because Jewish families usually spend Sabbath evenings together.

The next day there were services all day. In the morning there was a very solemn moment when the **Yizkor** prayer was

11

recited in memory of relatives and members of the congregation who had died. They were each mentioned by name, and their families and friends promised to give contributions, in their names, to people who were in need of help. The rabbi also asked everyone to remember the Jews who had died in the concentration camps, and also the young soldiers who had died while fighting for the new State of Israel.

*Synagogue interior with the bimah in the foreground*

Mr Singer and David stayed at the synagogue all day, but Miriam went for a walk in the park with Paul in the afternoon, and their mother took Gran home for a rest.

During the afternoon David's mind sometimes wandered, and he often felt very hungry. But one thing he enjoyed was the reading in the synagogue of the Book of Jonah. Jonah was a prophet who thought that God should only forgive Jews; he tried to run away when God told him to help non-Jews find forgiveness. But God showed him that He loved everyone, and wanted to forgive everyone.

12

All the family attended the final service, the **Neilah**. The rabbi asked God to bless everyone with health and happiness during the coming year, and to give them many opportunities to help others. Finally he said, "Blessed be the name of His Glorious Kingdom for ever and ever."

"The Lord, He is God," the congregation replied.

The cantor blew the shofar. Darkness had fallen outside the synagogue. Yom Kippur was over for another year.

After supper David said, "Tell me again about what happened in the Temple on Yom Kippur."

"Well," said his father, "before the Romans ruled Jerusalem there had been many faithful high priests. Simon the Just, for example, was called 'great among his brethren and the glory of his people'. He had urged men to follow the Torah and to serve God, showing mercy to one another. The Romans, however, sometimes appointed someone to be high priest because he would co-operate with them, and not because he was a holy man.

"Yom Kippur was an anxious time for such a high priest. Many of the services in the Temple were celebrated without him, but for a whole week before this festival he lived in the Temple and performed all the sacrifices. Meanwhile, the priests helped him learn the special Torah readings for the feast. This was very important, because if he made a mistake on Yom Kippur he would be disqualified, and an understudy would take his place for the rest of the day.

"On the night of the festival the high priest wasn't allowed to sleep. To keep him awake, the priests made him discuss the scriptures and sing psalms. They even made him walk up and down on the cold stone floors in bare feet! At daybreak they dressed him in his magnificent robes."

"I know," said Paul. "He had an elaborate head-dress and a breastplate decorated with twelve jewels, one for each of the twelve tribes of Israel. Golden bells were stitched to his robes. Our teacher says this explains why we decorate our scrolls with so many symbols."

13

*Part of a model of Jerusalem, showing how the Temple would have looked around the time of Jesus. The Holy of Holies is inside the tall Sanctuary building in the background, which stands in the Court of the Priests. In front of this is the Court of the Women. Next comes the double Court of the Israelites. In the foreground are the Court of the Gentiles and the Susa Gate.*

"Good, Paul. The high priest then burnt incense and lit the great candlestick, or **menorah**. Afterwards he bathed and put on a plain white linen robe, a symbol that he wished to be rid of his sins.

"During the services a bull and a goat were sacrificed. Another goat — the scapegoat — was driven outside the city and killed. Do you know why?"

"Yes," said Miriam. "Long ago people believed that when God forgave you He transferred your sins to another person or to an animal. And the crowds who worshipped at the Temple gradually came to see the scapegoat as a symbol that God had forgiven them."

"That's right. Then the high priest prayed for forgiveness for himself and his family, the priests and their families, and

14

lastly for the people and their families. Finally he went into the most sacred part of the Temple, the **Holy of Holies**, and again prayed for forgiveness."

"And that was the only time in the whole year that anyone entered the room," said David.

As they were washing up, Miriam asked her mother, "Ought we to celebrate Yom Kippur today, when we haven't got a temple or a high priest?"

"Remember that even when the Temple was standing, many Jews didn't go to Jerusalem. They prayed and fasted in their own synagogues, talking to God themselves."

Gran put down the plates she had been drying. "Your grandfather liked to tell the story of Rabbi Jochanan and his pupil, Rabbi Joshua. They were standing in the ruins of the Temple. Rabbi Joshua was very upset because the place where the high priest used to ask for God's forgiveness had been destroyed. Rabbi Jochanan told him, 'Don't be so sad. Remember how God told the prophets that living good lives was more important than sacrificing animals. God will always forgive us if we help other people.'"

David put his head round the kitchen door. "And remember the story of the rabbi in Eastern Europe who missed the Kol Nidre service because he was taking a stray cow back to its non-Jewish owner."

Suddenly he looked sheepish. "Any more to eat?"

# 3

# To Hate — or to Forgive

After the match, David and his friends walked up from the football pitch. As it was Wednesday evening he'd been able to play in the team. But, in spite of the fact that he'd scored two goals, they'd lost the game. The boys had a quick shower and collected some tins of Coke.

Sitting on the pavilion steps, watching David munch biscuit after biscuit, his friend, John, said, "Everyone can tell you fasted yesterday!" He suddenly became serious. "Didn't you say that your festival was to do with asking people's forgiveness?"

David, his mouth full, just nodded.

"Well, there was a film on TV last night about a Jewish family in Holland during the last war. All of them were sent to a concentration camp. I didn't see any of the guards asking them for forgiveness. And I can't imagine God wanting to forgive those guards, either. Didn't some of your grandmother's family die in one of the camps?"

"Mm . . . everyone except Gran herself, and my father. Only last night they were arguing about whether we should still try to track down Nazi war criminals and punish them, or forgive them and leave them alone. You see, Yom Kippur's about forgiving as well as being forgiven."

"Well, would you forgive them?"

"I'm not sure. Nobody's ever really hurt me — intentionally I mean!" David looked ruefully down at two large bruises on his left leg, the results of a hefty tackle! "Nobody's ever called me names at school, or in the street. We're told at synagogue classes that we must forgive others — but I just don't know whether I would forgive the Nazis or not."

16

"Would you forgive them if they hurt your mother and father – or young Paul? If anyone hurt my family I'd want to go on punishing them for the rest of their lives! It would only be fair. If we don't punish bullies, they will go on thinking they can do whatever they like."

"We believe in a God of justice as well as a God of forgiveness," David replied. "At synagogue classes we often read stories about God punishing evil. I don't think forgiving means that you don't punish people. You do punish them – not by yourself of course, but by handing them over to the police. After the war, a lot of Jews wanted their prison guards punished – but I think they forgave them."

"But the guards weren't tortured! I think they should have been made to feel what it was like."

"The rabbi said that would have been revenge, not justice. He said it's right to hate what people do, but not to hate the people themselves. If we'd tortured the Nazi guards, we would have been no better than they were."

"But it must be very hard not to hate." John paused. "You know, after Mass a few weeks ago our priest told us the same thing. But he was talking about some African guerrilla fighters who had killed two of our missionaries at a Catholic school."

David hesitated. "Gran said that in the concentration camps prisoners of many religions refused to hate their captors. And that was why they didn't become bitter and miserable, but were still kind and loving people when they were released."

The boys collected the empty Coke cans and went back into the pavilion, deep in thought.

While they were having tea, David told the family about his talk with John. After he'd gone upstairs to do his homework, Miriam said, "I think David coped very well."

Mr Singer smiled. "He's beginning to understand what a Jew believes and feels about things."

Miriam frowned. "I feel very muddled. We were talking about war and killing at the youth club last week. The rabbi said that some Jews believe that *all* killing is wrong. If God

17

made everyone, it's wrong for us ever to kill each other and we ought to find other ways of fighting evil."

"I know," said her mother. "But countless Jews remember the many brave men in the past who fought so that Jews could have the right to live and worship as they chose. They feel it right to fight against evil, when all other attempts to gain justice have failed."

Mr Singer sighed. "In every religion, there are some people who believe it right to fight – as a last resort – and others who feel it is always wrong to fight. Perhaps questions about love and hatred and the preciousness of life are the hardest ones we ever have to try to answer. A good Jew must always be prepared to rethink what he believes about loving and hating, and acting responsibly."

He paused. "I'm going to tell you what one of our great teachers once said a long time ago. You may not fully understand it at the moment, but try to remember it.

"He said we mustn't take revenge but always show compassion. We must seek justice for our enemies but we must also seek justice for ourselves, otherwise some people will never learn to act responsibly and will always do what they like. And when we do punish people, we must always remember that God is their Father too. He grieves for them and tells us to love the wicked as if they were our brothers!"

There was a long pause while Miriam thought about what her father had said. "Should people stop writing about the war with Germany then, and try to forget all the bad things that happened?"

"No. Knowledge of the past helps us to guard against allowing such things to happen again. We can all be cruel at times. And we should also remember the courage and love and bravery shown by the prisoners of the Nazis. Their example helps us to understand what religion is all about. As Ben Gurion, the first prime minister of the new State of Israel, said, 'Forgive, but never forget.'"

"But didn't some Jews feel that God had let them down? Or that He didn't exist at all?"

18

"A few did. But many people – not only Jews – kept their faith, and through their courage showed that evil can never conquer goodness. God has a purpose for the world, and no one can stop that purpose being fulfilled."

"That sounds very strange. But I'll think about it."

Mrs Singer put her hand on her daughter's shoulder.

"I once heard someone say that God's purpose for the world is like a jigsaw puzzle. All the pieces can't be found in the box we call earth. Some are with God in Heaven. Trusting in God means believing that He has those pieces."

# 4
# Succoth:
# The Festival of Tabernacles

"Pass me up another of those branches."

Mr Singer was putting the roof on the **succah** (tabernacle), a small makeshift room built against the back wall of the house. Two sides were made of plywood and the third of trellis. Mrs Singer was hanging curtains and mats over the wood to make it look more colourful.

The roof had to be made of something which had grown from the earth. A neighbour had given David some branches from a tree he'd chopped down in his garden. When the last branch was in place, David's father told him to check carefully to make sure that they could see the sky clearly between the leaves.

Miriam helped her mother decorate the succah with apples, oranges, grapes, tomatoes, sweet corn, little boxes of sweets and flour and small bottles of oil and water. David put pictures of Israel on the walls. He'd cut them out of travel brochures. Paul pinned up some of his own paintings. One showed Moses and the Israelites travelling in the wilderness. Another showed an Israelite family building a succah in the desert where they would sleep for the night.

"It looks smashing," said Paul, reaching for a grape, only to have his hand slapped by his grandmother.

"You know very well that the decorations mustn't be eaten until the festival is over."

20

*Succoth are often beautifully decorated, in accordance with God's command that the festival should be celebrated "with joy".*

Paul began to look cross, so Miriam quickly changed the subject. "I went to see Susan's succah at lunch-time. Her father has emptied out the garden shed, and they've decorated it. You turn a handle on the wall, the roof swings back and you put branches over the space."

Paul looked interested. "Why can't we have one like that, Dad?"

"Like many Jews, I prefer to build my own succah each year," his father answered. "Of course, it's not easy to do that if you live in a large block of flats in a city, or if you have no garden. I've seen succahs built on roof-tops, over garages or fire escapes – I've even seen a picture of some Jewish soldiers building one on the back of an army lorry! Many synagogues build a communal succah. If a family has no place to build

21

*Sharing a meal in a succah*

their own succah, they can take the food to the synagogue and eat it there."

"We've got a succah in our playground," Paul said. "Some of the older boys from the synagogue built it after school last night and Class Two decorated it this afternoon."

Gran had been quietly putting some finishing touches to the decorations. Now she unpacked the small cardboard box in which the **etrog** (citron) lay, looking like a fat, juicy lemon. She put it on the table with the **lulav** (palm branches), and the branches of myrtle and willow. These are called the four symbols of **Succoth**. Carefully Mr Singer bound all the branches together. Now they were ready to use in the synagogue service later in the week.

Paul's class were very excited when they went into Assembly on the day before Succoth. First, the Headmaster told the story of how Moses and the Israelites built succahs in the wilderness to protect them from heat and cold.

"Gradually the people began to understand how dependent they were on God's gifts. And so, for one week in every year, we spend at least part of each day in our own succahs and eat our meals there – to remind us that we also depend on God's care. Succoth is a harvest festival too, reminding us that without God's gifts of sun and rain, all the efforts of the farmers to produce food would be useless."

One of the teachers then described the celebrations in Jerusalem under the Romans. She told how people came from many towns and cities, some travelling very long distances. When they caught their first glimpse of the Temple, they shouted for joy and sang psalms, like the one beginning: "I was glad when they said unto me, let us go into the house of the Lord." The people built booths in every available space and Jerusalem began to look like a huge park.

Then everyone hurried to the Temple. They followed the high priest to the pool of Siloam, where he filled a golden pitcher with water. The procession wound its way back to the great stone altar. As the priests blew silver trumpets and sang psalms, the people waved willow branches, and the high priest poured the water on to the altar.

In the evening four tall menorah (candlesticks) were lit in the Court of the Women. There was singing and dancing and the men juggled with lighted torches.

The festivities continued for a whole week. On the seventh day, when the water was poured on the altar, the people walked round it seven times beating the willow branches on the ground and praying for rain, to help bring good harvests.

When the teacher had finished speaking, four children stepped to the front of the platform, each carrying one of the four symbols. They spoke in turn.

"I am etrog, the citron. I represent fire."

"I am lulav, the palm branch. I grow straight up into the sky. I represent air."

"I am myrtle, I grow close to the earth. I represent earth."

"I am willow, I grow beside water. I represent water."

*Jewish children holding the symbols of the harvest, the etrog and the lulav*

Together they said: 'We are the four elements. Without us nothing exists. We were created by God."

Four more children took their place.

"I am etrog, shaped like a heart. I love God."

"I am lulav, straight like a spine. I serve God."

"I am myrtle, with leaves like eyes. I read the Torah."

"I am willow, with leaves like lips. I praise God."

"Together we make up the human body. Every part of us serves God."

The children joined hands to form two groups. "At Succoth we, the four symbols, are bound together and waved in the air. Let us all combine our different gifts to help each other."

On the first day of the festival, Paul went with his family to the synagogue. His father carried the four symbols, being very careful not to damage any of them.

In his sermon the rabbi reminded them that the name Jew is a shortened form of Judah which means "thanks to the Lord". Today they were especially remembering to thank God for taking care of them.

The cantor took a scroll from the Ark. Standing on the bimah, he lifted it up as high as he could. All the congregation walked round the bimah, saying, "Save us we pray". Then Mr Singer, and all the other people carrying the four symbols, waved the plants to the north, south, east, west and up and down. Paul knew that this was to show that although Jews lived all over the world, doing all kinds of jobs, God cared for them all.

# THINGS TO DO, THINGS TO DISCUSS

Chapters 1–4

1 Find out about the history of the Jewish people from reference books and encyclopaedias. What parts did Abraham, Moses, David and Solomon, for example, play in the establishment of the Jewish religion?

2 Find out all you can about the Temple at Jerusalem under Roman rule. How were the festivals celebrated there? Imagine you are making a pilgrimage to Jerusalem to celebrate one of these festivals. Describe your visit in a poem or an essay, or through a painting.

3 In what ways do different religious communities seek to help people? (Look for examples in a copy of the *Jewish Chronicle*.) Do you think more could be done? If so, make a list of suggestions.

4 In the light of what you have read, organize a class discussion on forgiveness. How can we show that we forgive people? Should we always forgive?

5 Many religions tell of a God who is loving and forgiving, and who, at the same time, is just and punishes people. What are your views on such beliefs? Organize a class debate to discuss them.

# 5

# Simchat Torah: Rejoicing in the Law

Miriam's schoolfriends had asked her if they could visit the synagogue. When she mentioned it at home, Mrs Singer said, "Why not invite them to the evening service on **Simchat Torah**? It's such a happy service. There's plenty to see and it would be much better than visiting an empty building."

The girls thought it was a great idea. "Isn't that the festival where you finish the reading of the Torah?" asked Miriam's teacher.

"Yes. Every Monday, Thursday and **Shabbat** – that's Saturday – we read verses from the Torah in the synagogue. We start with the first verse of **Genesis** and end with the last verse of **Deuteronomy**. It takes exactly a year to read it all. But on Simchat Torah we don't only celebrate the fact that we've finished reading it. That might look as if we were glad that at last we'd got to the end. We also read the first verses of the Torah at the same service, to show that we look forward to hearing it all again."

"What exactly *is* the Torah?" asked Miriam's friend, Jane.

"The Torah, or Law, is made up of the first five books of the Christian Old Testament: Genesis, **Exodus**, Leviticus, Numbers and Deuteronomy. We call it the Book of Moses, because it contains the story of Moses and the laws which God revealed to him for the people."

"Don't you read the other parts of the Christian Bible?"

"Oh, yes. In the synagogue we never read the Christian New Testament, but we *do* read many other books of the Old

27

Testament. We divide these into two sections. The first is called the **Prophets**. There you'll find not only the messages of prophets like Amos and Isaiah, but also stories of the early judges, and an account of the history of the early kingdoms of Israel and Judah. The other section is called the **Writings**. This contains poetry like the psalms, wise sayings, and some stories, for example those of Ruth, Esther and Job."

"Haven't I heard you mention other books?" Miriam's teacher asked.

"Well, there is the **Apocrypha**. Father says Christians often read this too. This is another collection of books and includes the story of the **Maccabees**, a brave family who fought for the Jews' right to worship in their own way. We read the story at the festival of **Chanukah**. Then there are many commentaries on the Torah by wise rabbis, telling us how we should live our lives, celebrate festivals, eat, behave towards other people, and so on. Many of these teachings are found in a book called the **Talmud**. We believe we must always keep on studying the Torah, trying to find new meanings in it. We say no one can ever learn all it has to teach."

"It seems very important to you," said Jane.

"It is. In times of persecution, Jews have often died rather than damage the scrolls on which the Law is written. If we didn't have the Law, we wouldn't know how God wants us to behave. The Torah is God's greatest gift to us, because it teaches us how to love Him and to love other people."

"I once saw a picture of a rabbi reading the Law in a synagogue," said another girl, "but he wasn't reading an ordinary book – it looked like a scroll."

"The Law is written by hand on pieces of parchment, which are fastened together to form a scroll," Miriam explained. "It's written in Hebrew and you need special training to become a Torah scribe. That's one reason why the scrolls are so expensive. They take a very long time to write."

The girls all arrived early at the synagogue. Mrs Singer met them at the door. She explained that in Orthodox synagogues

28

*Taking a scroll out of the Ark*

women and men sit separately, and then she led them upstairs to the balcony.

As the girls watched closely, all the scrolls were taken from the Ark and given to members of the congregation. Each one was carried seven times round the bimah in procession and all the congregation joined in. Like many other boys and girls, Paul waved a flag that he'd made at school and David carried a small copy of the Torah which he'd been given on his last birthday. Miriam's friends noticed that the scrolls often changed hands. Mrs Singer told them that this meant that as

29

*In the synagogue the reader follows the words of the Torah with a pointer, called a yad, to avoid touching the scroll.*

many people as possible could have the honour of carrying them.

Miriam whispered, "In Jerusalem people join long processions which wind through the streets to the Western Wall. They carry the scrolls under canopies or talliths, and they dance in the streets."

"People usually dance in the synagogues too," added her mother.

After the service, Miriam took her friends to the adjoining hall, where all the young people were given fruit and sweets. Soon her brothers joined them.

David commented, "There's another service in the morning."

"Will it be the same as tonight's?"

"Not quite. Three members of the congregation will carry scrolls from the Ark to the bimah. It is a very great honour to be chosen to read from them at Simchat Torah. The last two chapters of Deuteronomy will be read and the congregation will reply, 'Be strong and let us be strengthened.'"

"We always repeat those words after the last verses have been read from any of the five books of the Torah," explained Mrs Singer.

David continued, "After the first two chapters of Genesis have been read, the congregation will recite, 'And this is the Torah that Moses placed before the children of Israel, by the command of the Lord, by the hand of Moses.' Then all men and boys over thirteen will go up to the bimah to recite the blessing over a reading. In some synagogues they say it individually – but here, thank goodness, we say it in groups."

"And," said Paul, "just before the rabbi gives the final blessing, all children under thirteen will go up to the bimah. The adults will hold up a tallith over us and we will say the blessing together. . . . Can I have another apple?"

# 6
# Miriam celebrates her Birthday

Jane walked slowly up the path towards the front door. She'd been invited to Miriam's birthday party, but she felt rather nervous, because this was the first time she'd visited a Jewish home.

As she rang the bell, she looked curiously at the small oblong box fastened to the right-hand doorpost.

Miriam opened the door. "That's a **mezuzah**," she said,

*The prayer written on the parchment inside a mezuzah begins with the Hebrew words "Shema Israel, Adonai, Elohenu, Adonai Echad!"*

noticing Jane's interest in the box. "It's made of wood, but it could be made of metal or stone. Inside there's a small piece of parchment with quotations from the book of Deuteronomy written on it."

Her father and Paul joined them. "Hello, Jane," said Mr Singer. "See if Paul can remember what the quotations are."

"One is part of our daily prayers called the **Shema**," said Paul. "It says, 'Hear, O Israel, the Lord our God is one. And thou shalt worship the Lord our God with all thy heart, and with all thy soul, and with all thy strength.'"

"And the other one?"

"It's something to do with parents teaching their children the Torah . . . I know – 'and write them (the laws) on the doorpost of your house.'"

"Right. Come in, Jane," said Mr Singer, "and I'll show you what a mezuzah is like inside." First he showed Jane the mezuzahs on the doors of the living-room and the study. Then he took a small cardboard box from his desk. Inside was a metal mezuzah. He opened the back and drew out the small scroll.

"Look. It's handwritten in black ink in Hebrew. The scribe, or **sofer**, writes with a quill."

"Why is there a small hole in the case?" asked Jane.

Paul broke in, "You fold the parchment very carefully, so that when it's slipped into the case you can see the word 'Almighty' through the hole." He turned to his sister. "Can you remember the little ceremony we had when we moved into this house?"

"Yes, I can. Dad recited some verses from Psalm 30. And then he said a prayer."

Quietly her father recited, "Grant that this family may live together in brotherhood and fellowship, and may they meditate on the Law and be faithful to Thy precepts."

"Then you fastened the mezuzah next to the front door," said Paul, "and after I'd gone to bed, you put some others on the doorposts of the living-room, study and bedrooms."

"Why do you do this?" asked Jane.

*Jews fix a mezuzah to right-hand doorposts to remind them to obey God both inside and outside their homes.*

"Quite simply because God told us to do so. And it shows everyone that this is a house where God is loved and obeyed."

While Miriam looked after her other guests, David showed Jane the two candlesticks they used each Shabbat and the beautiful eight-branched menorah kept for the festival of Chanukah. Mrs Singer brought out the lovely cloths that were put over the bread and wine at ceremonial meals and she also showed Jane a beautiful **Passover** plate.

Then Mr Singer showed her his prayer shawl, or tallith, and two little boxes called **tefillin**. He explained that he wore these every weekday when he was praying, but added that tefillin are not normally worn on Shabbat.

As they looked at the long white shawl with black stripes at either end, Jane asked about the knotted fringes.

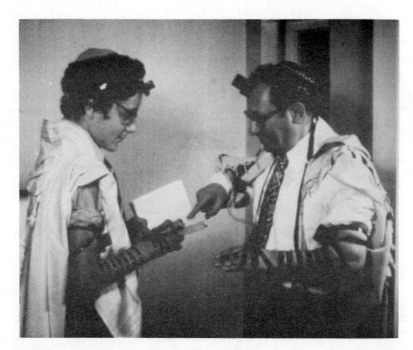

*This boy is left-handed, so he wears his tefillin on his right arm.*

"These help us to remember to obey the Law," said Mr Singer.

"Does Miriam have a tallith?"

"No, only boys over thirteen and men wear them. David will wear one after his next birthday."

Jane was very puzzled by the tefillin, two square black boxes attached to long leather thongs. Mr Singer put them on to show her how he wore them. He fastened one to the upper part of his left arm, facing towards the heart. The straps were fastened round his forearm, hand and middle finger. "This shows that I love the Law and will obey it," he told her. Then he fastened the other one just above his forehead and knotted the straps at the back of his head. "This reminds me to *think* about the Law."

Paul came in and showed her his **capel** or **yarmulka**, a small skull-cap. "Men and boys wear them when they pray. It's a mark of respect to God. Some of my friends wear them all the time."

Miriam called Jane into the kitchen, where she was very intrigued to see *two* sink units! Miriam explained the reason for this.

"We have a lot of traditions about what food to eat and how to prepare it. We don't eat meat and milk foods together. We use separate sets of cutlery for them and have two sinks for the washing-up."

"So you can't have roast beef and then rice pudding?"

"No. We can't even have milk in our tea, if we're eating meat."

"You don't eat pork or bacon, do you?"

"No. The foods we can eat are called kosher, or permitted foods. All the meat we eat must come from animals killed in a special way, called **Shechita**, where as much blood as possible is drained away from the animal's body. Some people say the way we kill animals is cruel. But the Law says that God created animals as well as people, and we must be kind to them too. We wouldn't let animals suffer any pain."

"Can you eat fish?"

"Yes – any fish with fins and scales. We can eat poultry, too."

"Where do you buy your food?"

"We buy things like fruit and vegetables anywhere. But meat comes from a special kosher butcher. Often large stores and supermarkets have a kosher section. One big difficulty is that many products – like cakes, bread, jellies, ice cream and washing-up liquid – may contain forbidden fats. So we always have to look carefully at the labels. Of course, if there's a kosher bakery near by, it's a great help."

"Why do you have all these rules?"

Mrs Singer, who was taking a tray of cakes out of the oven, said, "Again, because it is God's law. And buying and preparing food takes a long time. All the care we have to take

*Food plays an important part in Jewish ritual observance. Jews may only eat kosher foods, prepared according to strict rules.*

reminds us constantly of God's presence and our promise to serve Him."

Paul put his head round the door and took one look at Jane's face. "Don't worry," he teased. "There's plenty to eat."

He led the way to the table, which was covered with plates of sandwiches, cakes, fruits and jellies. And in the middle was a large birthday cake with fifteen candles.

Everyone waited quietly while Mr Singer said a short blessing, thanking God for the gift of food.

# 7
# Shabbat:
# The Sabbath

David and Paul tidied away their books and games. It was Friday, and at sunset Shabbat would begin. Gran always talked about it as "the Sabbath Queen" and insisted that they prepared for the Sabbath as if they were preparing for a visit from a very important person. Mrs Singer had cleaned the house, Miriam had polished the two Sabbath candlesticks, and now they were preparing the evening meal. No ordinary work was permitted on Shabbat, so all the cooking had to be finished by tea-time.

*Hallah cover embroidered with pictures of objects used in the celebration of the Sabbath*

Gran covered the table with a snowy-white cloth. She put the candles into their holders, and brought two freshly baked braided loaves called **hallot** from the kitchen. There were *two* loaves, to remind them that, in the wilderness, on the day before Shabbat the Israelites had gathered two portions of manna.

When Mr Singer arrived home he found that he had just enough time to telephone a friend (he didn't use the telephone on Shabbat). Then, after they'd washed and changed into clean clothes, David and Paul went with their father to the evening service to welcome the Shabbat. They all wore their capels. When he had bought their house, Mr Singer had made sure that it was within walking distance of the synagogue, for he never drove his car on Shabbat.

At home, Miriam put the weekly family contribution into a collecting box to help buy a kidney machine for the local hospital. Then she stood quietly by the dining-room table with her mother and grandmother.

Mrs Singer prayed that God would take care of her family, and that the children would grow up to love and obey the Law: "Grant that peace, light and joy ever abide in our home." She lit the candles, covered her eyes with her hands, and welcomed the Sabbath into their home.

"Blessed art Thou, Lord our God, King of the Universe, who has sanctified us with the Commandments and com- manded us to kindle the Sabbath lights," she prayed, and as the candle-light spread across the room, it seemed to fill it with warmth and joy.

"Shabbat Shalom – a peaceful Sabbath." Mr Singer had re- turned with the boys. He blessed the children, saying to David and Paul, "May God make you as Ephraim and Manasseh," and to Miriam, "May God make you as Sarah, Rebecca, Rachel and Leah." Putting his hands on their heads, he said, "May the Lord bless you and protect you . . . and grant you peace." Finally, he thanked God for his wife, who had created a home where God was always present.

*The father of the family says the kiddush blessing.*

*Silver kiddush cup. The drinking of wine from the kiddush cup emphasizes the joy of Jewish worship.*

Then he filled the **kiddush** cup (the cup of sanctification) with wine, and blessed it, reminding them that God had created everything before resting on the Sabbath day.

After pouring water over their hands, everyone sat down at the table. Mr Singer blessed the hallot. Then he cut one loaf into slices and passed it round. Everyone took a piece and ate it.

Mrs Singer brought in the meal of fish, chicken and fruit. As they ate, they sang many traditional songs called **Zmirot.**

Feeding the world like a Shepherd,
Father whose bread we have eaten,
Father whose wine we have drunk,
Now to His name we are singing,
Praising Him loud with our voices.

The meal ended with a prayer, thanking God for His gifts.

Next morning, the family went to the synagogue. Paul went into a separate room, designed as a children's synagogue, where there was a special service. David and his father sat downstairs, and Miriam went to the gallery with her mother and grandmother. She looked around her. On the eastern wall was the **Aron Hakodesh**, the Ark. Facing it, she faced the city of Jerusalem.

Inside the Ark were the scrolls of the Law, written on parchment by the sofer. They were wrapped in covers of many colours, but white covers were used at Rosh Hashanah and Yom Kippur. The covers were embroidered with many Jewish symbols – there were lions and crowns, representing kingship, candlesticks, and tablets of stone, representing those given to Moses on which were written the Ten Commandments. Over the covers hung metal breastplates, symbolizing the one worn by the high priest in the Temple. Each had a headpiece shaped like a crown, to which bells were attached. When the bells rang, they reminded people of the bells sewn on to the hem of the high priest's ceremonial robes, and they called them to hear the word of the Torah. For each scroll there was a silver

41

*Children's synagogue*

rod, ending in the shape of a hand. This was a **yad**, which was used as a pointer by those reading the lessons.

Covering the Ark was a velvet curtain, a **Parochet**, which Miriam's mother had helped to make and embroider. Above it were paintings of the tablets of stone given to Moses on Mount Sinai and one of the Star of David. This star consists of two interlaced triangles. It has been found on Jewish buildings and tombstones dating from about the sixth century C.E. No one knows its real origin, but it has become a symbol of Judaism.

Hanging in front of the Ark was the **Ner Tamid**, a light which was always left burning. In the Temple, it had represented God's presence. Here, in the synagogue, it showed that the light of God's teaching and love would always be spread by the community.

The service was conducted from a platform, or bimah, in front of the Ark.

*Torah scrolls wrapped in embroidered mantles with silver breastplates*

Light streamed into the synagogue through a number of windows, many made of stained glass. These were decorated with symbols representing the different Jewish festivals. But there were no human figures, for the Law says, "Thou shalt not make unto thyself any graven image."

The service began. Miriam followed it in her prayer book, or **Siddur**. The Hebrew and English words were written side by side. She enjoyed listening to the cantor leading the prayers and the singing. He had a beautiful, rich, baritone voice.

Miriam's father had been chosen to carry the scroll from the Ark to the bimah for the reading from the Law. This was a great honour. The rabbi read the lesson in Hebrew, following the text with the yad. When he had finished, he carefully replaced the cover, the breastplate and the **keter** (crown) and Mr Singer carefully carried the scroll back to the Ark.

The lesson from the Prophets was read by a young man who

43

The silver headpieces that fit over the Torah rollers are called rimmonim. The bells call people to listen to God's word.

Ner Tamid hanging in front of the Ark. The Ark and the parochet are decorated with symbolic images.

Havdalah ceremony

44

was soon to be married. Miriam remembered that David would read the lesson from the Prophets at his bar-mitzvah.

In his short sermon the rabbi told them that God rested on the Sabbath day, not because He was tired, but so that they might follow His example. Human beings were the stewards of the rest of the creation and of each other and they must remember to care for that creation, giving everyone and everything love and dignity. When they rested on the Sabbath they had more time to remember God and think about His will for them.

After a light lunch, Mr and Mrs Singer went to visit friends, while Gran had a rest. David played chess with Paul, and Miriam went to a meeting for young people at the synagogue. They chatted and sang folk-songs and also made plans for a sponsored swim and a sponsored walk to raise money for the Jewish Association for the Blind.

David went with his father to the evening service. "A good week," they called to their friends as they returned home. It was a clear night and they could actually count the first three stars to appear in the sky. Shabbat was coming to an end.

At home, everyone gathered round for the **Havdalah** ceremony. Havdalah means "separation", the separation of the Sabbath from the coming week. First, Mr Singer blessed the cup of wine, praying that the week would be full of joy. Miriam passed round the spice box, and they all smelled the contents. These represented the happy atmosphere which they hoped would remain in the house for the next six days. Paul held the blue and white Havdalah candle, while his father prayed that the light of God's presence would remain with then until the next Shabbat:

"Blessed art Thou, O Lord, King of the Universe, who makest a division between the holy and the ordinary, between light and darkness, between the seventh day and working days."

Carefully, Paul snuffed out the flame in the wine cup. Shabbat was over.

# 8
# Chanukah:
# The Festival of Dedication

David settled down to his homework. Tonight he had to write an essay on courage, and he'd decided to write about one of the great Jewish leaders of the past. In three days' time they would be celebrating the festival of **Chanukah**, when they remembered the great patriot, Judas Maccabeus.

Over two thousand years ago Judas had led his family and his Jewish countrymen in a revolt against their cruel Syrian conquerors. The Syrian king had forbidden the Jews to worship God in their traditional ways. He said that if they kept the Sabbath, celebrated their festivals, or read the Torah, they would be put to death. Then he ordered them to eat forbidden pigs' flesh and he turned their Temple at Jerusalem into a temple for heathen worship.

Judas's father was the priest in the village of Modi'in, near modern Tel Aviv. When he heard about the new laws, he said, "Even if all the nations within the King's Empire listen to him and give up their own faith, yet will I and my sons and my brothers follow the Covenant of our fathers. God forbid that we give up the Torah and the Commandments."

The revolution began, and after three years' fighting, the Jewish patriots captured Jerusalem. They immediately cleansed the Temple, removing all evidence of idol worship, and re-dedicated it to the worship of God. Jews were free to worship in their own way again.

David's father found the story for him in the Book of the Maccabees. After reading it carefully, David wrote out the story in his own words, then sat, sucking his pen.

"What's the matter?" asked Mr Singer.

"I can't think of a good ending."

"Why not explain that Judas's victory has come to represent all the victories of the Jews over tyrants who've tried to destroy us and our faith?"

"Mm . . . that's a good idea. Thanks, Dad."

Meanwhile, in the kitchen, Paul's mother was reminding him why they celebrated the festival for eight days, and why they used an eight-branched candlestick, or **Chanukiah**. (On the first evening they would light one candle from the servant candle, the **shamash**, on the second two candles, on the third three candles, and so on, until all eight candles were lit.)

*The Chanukiah is an important symbol of hope to Jewish families.*

It was all because of a beautiful legend about Judas's rededication of the Temple. It was said that when the soldiers came to light the great menorah, whose light represented God's presence with them, they found, to their dismay, that there was only one small jar of purified oil left, enough to burn for just one day. Remarkably, even though it took eight days to get fresh supplies of oil, the lamps never went out.

"And so," said Paul, "we light eight candles at Chanukah."

He told his mother about the Chanukiah he was helping to make at school. It was made of nine simple clay lamps fastened to a piece of wood. Eight would bear the names of countries where children were suffering because of war, oppression and hunger. The shamash lamp from which the others were lit would bear the words of the psalm which the Maccabean soldiers sang at their rededication ceremony.

The Chanukiah was for the people living at the Jewish old people's home near to the school. Each evening, after they'd lit their own candles in the class-room, Paul's class would go to visit the old people, many of whom had no families of their own. They'd light the candles, sing songs with them and, on the first evening, give them small gifts. On the last evening, Paul was to read a special Chanukah prayer, telling the story of Judas and his family. David had promised to help him learn it off by heart.

As darkness fell on the first evening of Chanukah, the family gathered round the beautiful silver Chanukiah which Mrs Singer's grandfather had brought from Poland. It stood on the window-ledge, so that everyone who passed by would be able to see the burning candles. Tonight Mr Singer would say the prayers, but everyone would take their turn during the week. He lit the shamash candle, then carefully lit the first Chanukah candle, quietly saying in Hebrew, "Blessed are You, O Lord our God, King of the Universe, who sanctified us with the Commandments and commanded us to kindle the Chanukah light."

The candle had to be left burning for half an hour, and during this time no work was done. The first evening was a time of great excitement, because there were presents for the children. All received small gifts of money, **Chanukah gelt**, from their grandmother. The coins symbolized the coins struck by the Maccabees when they captured Jerusalem. There were presents from their parents too. For Miriam there was a copy of *The Hanukkah Book*, which told her all she would need to know to celebrate the festival properly when she had a house of her own. Paul curled up in front of the fire with a book full of Chanukah games to play and models to make. And David was delighted with his new cassette tape. There was a play about the rededication of the Temple on one side, and there were songs and stories for each evening of the festival on the other.

While Mr Singer and Miriam prepared the evening meal, Paul persuaded the rest of the family to play a special game with a **dreidel**, a kind of spinning-top. Some Jews say the game was copied from one played by German Christians on Christmas Eve, but others say it was one of the games kept on the table with the Torah at times when Jews were forbidden to read their scriptures. If any soldiers or police arrived, they could pretend they'd merely been amusing themselves.

*Dreidel*

Soon Miriam called them to the table. Paul was very pleased to see a plate of his favourite **latkes**, a traditional treat from Poland. There were also doughnuts, a favourite Chanukah dish in Israel. Both of these foods were cooked in oil to remind them of the oil which had burned in the menorah lamps over two thousand years ago.

Gran told Paul that in South America Jews would be celebrating with chick-pea stew, in Greece with beef casserole, in Holland with roast goose stuffed with apples, and in India with rice and lentil pilafs. Paul's mouth watered as he listened!

As the meal came to an end, they sang traditional songs, including one called "O Fortress, Rock of my Salvation", which was probably written in Germany in the thirteenth century. As well as telling the story of Chanukah, this song gives thanks to God for delivering the Jews from many dangers, and looks forward to the coming of the Messiah.

*Primary school children lighting their Chanukiah*

The week of Chanukah was a very busy one for Miriam. Her teacher had asked her to organize the Assemblies for the Upper School, using the theme of the festival. On four mornings, she and her friends read from the story of Judas, telling not only of the rebellion and the rededication of the Temple, but also of Hannah, who encouraged her seven sons to die rather than deny their Jewish faith. Each morning, after the reading, the girls lit a candle and asked everyone to think about people in the world who were suffering.

On Friday morning, Miriam described how the festival is celebrated in Israel. Thousands of young people gather round a huge bonfire in Modi'in. Torches are lit and carried by relay teams to every city and town, and to the Western Wall in Jerusalem, the only surviving part of the old Temple wall. Finally Miriam asked everyone to pledge themselves to do everything they could to make sure people everywhere should always be free to worship in their own way.

# THINGS TO DO, THINGS TO DISCUSS

Chapters 5–8

1 If there is a synagogue near your school, arrange to visit it. It may be possible to be shown round the building by the rabbi, and also to attend a service. Some members of the group might take photographs, and others could write a commentary to explain them.

2 If such a visit is not possible, try to borrow a filmstrip about a synagogue or one showing Jewish ritual objects. Perhaps your school, or one nearby, has a video tape of the programme on Judaism in the ATV schools series *Believe it or not*. You could also ask a Jewish visitor to talk to you about his home and his synagogue.

3 Make your own recording about one of the Jewish festivals, explaining why the festival is important to a Jew. (*Enjoy Chanukah at Home* and *Enjoy Purim at Home*, cassettes available from the Jewish Education Bureau, may give you some ideas. See the Resources section for details.)

4 Design a Chanukiah. Write a prayer or prayers to recite as you light the candles.

5 Read some of the stories in the Torah. Why are these important to a Jew?

# 9
# A Wedding in the Family

Miriam was very excited. It was Sunday – and she was going to a wedding. Today her cousin, Chaim, was to marry Sarah, a girl he'd first met at the youth club.

Most of the guests had arrived when the Singer family reached the synagogue. The bridal canopy, or **chuppah**, which had been set up in front of the Ark, looked very beautiful. It was made of rich blue velvet, and embroidered along the front edge in Hebrew were the words: "Blessed art Thou, O Lord, who makes the bridegroom to rejoice with the bride."

The four supporting poles were covered with flowers.

"Gran arranged those yesterday afternoon," whispered Mrs Singer.

Miriam knew that the chuppah represented the home that Chaim and Sarah would build together. Her mother always stressed the importance of the Jewish home. Here festivals were celebrated, prayers were said, and children gradually learned what it meant to be a Jew. She remembered her father saying that many people had tried to stamp out Judaism by destroying synagogues and forbidding Jews to meet together for worship. But they had always failed because Judaism lived on in each Jewish home.

"Where's Chaim?" whispered Paul.

"He's in the rabbi's study with two of his friends. He's signing the marriage contract, the **ketubah**."

"Why aren't you there, Dad?"

"Because the two witnesses mustn't be related to either the bride or the groom."

Just then, Chaim and his father came in and stood beneath the chuppah. The rabbi and the cantor followed.

"Have you got to be married by a rabbi?" whispered Paul.

"It's the custom," his father replied. "And in Britain a marriage performed by a rabbi is accepted by law."

The cantor began the service: "Blessed be the one that cometh in the name of the Lord."

Everyone turned round so that they could watch Sarah and her father walk down the aisle. Behind them were her mother, Chaim's mother, the bridesmaid and the best man. Sarah wore a simple white dress and her face was covered by a veil. She hadn't wanted to wear anything elaborate. Miriam grinned to herself. It was lucky, she thought, that they didn't live in some of the Middle Eastern communities, where the bride wore a very exotic, richly embroidered costume, borrowed for the occasion.

*The chuppah is the unique feature of a Jewish wedding.*

As Sarah came to stand beside Chaim, the cantor chanted:
"He who is mighty, blessed and great above all beings,
May He bless the bridegroom and the bride."

The rabbi gave a short sermon, and then the cantor recited the blessings from the betrothal ceremony.

"What's a betrothal?" asked Paul.

"It's another name for an engagement," anwered his father. "The betrothal used to take place a year before the wedding, but today we usually celebrate the betrothal and the wedding together."

Chaim and Sarah took a sip of wine from the cup the rabbi held out to them. Paul tugged his father's sleeve again.

Mr Singer smiled and said, "Why do we drink wine on Shabbat?"

"Because it shows we are all happy on Shabbat," Paul replied.

"Well, Chaim and Sarah are drinking wine to tell us that their home will be full of happiness and joy!"

Chaim slipped a plain gold ring on to the forefinger of Sarah's right hand and said, "Behold, thou art consecrated unto me by this ring according to the law of Moses and Israel."

As Miriam watched, she remembered Gran telling her that many years ago wedding rings were often very elaborate, forming part of the bride's dowry. Today plain rings are used to show that rich and poor are all equal before God.

Chaim then read out the ketubah. He promised to love Sarah and to take care of her always.

The cantor recited the seven blessings as Chaim and Sarah took another sip of wine. He asked God the Creator, who had created man in His own image, to grant the bride and groom much happiness.

"Blessed are Thou, O Lord our God, King of the Universe, who has created joy and gladness, the bridegroom and the bride . . . pleasure and delight . . . brotherhood, peace and fellowship."

Someone had put an empty wineglass near Chaim's foot.

*Present-day Israeli Orthodox ketubah*

Suddenly, he crushed it with his heel. Paul gasped, vividly remembering his mother's comments when he'd dropped two of her Sabbath wineglasses.

His father put a hand on his shoulder and whispered, "That's to remind us that we must all learn to accept sorrow as well as happiness in our lives. And it also reminds us of the great tragedy of the destruction of our Temple by the Romans. Remember how often we speak of this in our prayers."

The service ended with a very familiar prayer: "The Lord bless you and keep you. The Lord make His face to shine upon you and be gracious unto you. The Lord lift up His countenance upon you and give you peace."

To cries of "Mazel Tov! Good luck!" the bride and groom left the synagogue. Talking and laughing, the guests, the cantor and the rabbi followed them to the wedding hall for the wedding reception.

*Sixteenth-century Italian ketubah*

They all had a wonderful time! The cantor said the blessing over the bread and the buffet meal began. Telegrams were read out. Speeches were made, and a very nervous Chaim said thank you to everyone.

When they'd all had a piece of wedding-cake, and no one, not even Paul, could eat any more, the cantor said grace and repeated once again the seven blessings for the bride and groom.

Then the chairs and tables were pushed back, and everyone joined in the singing and dancing. They all enjoyed listening to Miriam and her friends singing some Israeli folk-songs, and some songs from *Fiddler on the Roof*.

"Mazel Tov," cried Paul wearily, as he went home to bed.

# 10
# Purim:
# A Festival of Hope

"Paul, will you hurry up! We'll be late for the service!"

Paul looked stubbornly at his father. "I'm not going without my rattle, my gregger. I made it at school this morning from two aluminium foil dishes stapled together. I put rice inside and drew Haman's face on the outside."

Mr Singer took him firmly by the shoulder. "You'll. . . ."

"It's all right, Dad," interrupted Miriam, "I've found it. It was in his satchel all the time!"

The story told at the festival of **Purim** happened nearly two and a half thousand years ago. King Ahasuerus of Persia was angry with his queen. He divorced her and married a beautiful young Jewish girl called Esther. But he didn't know that she was a Jewess.

Haman, the King's chief minister, hated the Jews. When Esther's cousin, Mordecai, refused to bow down to him – for Mordecai would only bow down before God – Haman was very angry. He persuaded the King that all the Jews were plotting against the throne and obtained a sealed decree giving him permission to put all the Jews in the Empire to death. He cast lots – purim – using stones to decide on the date of the massacre. That's why the festival is called Purim.

Esther heard of Haman's plot. She knew that if anyone entered the King's presence without being sent for, he would be put to death. But she bravely went to the throne-room and her husband not only forgave her, but said he would grant any favour she asked.

Esther invited the King and Haman to a feast. While they were eating, she told the King of Haman's wickedness and said that, because she was a Jewess, she too would be killed.

Ahasuerus was very angry. He ordered Haman to be put to death. But what of the Jews? Any law passed by a Persian king must be carried out. Suddenly he had an idea. Warnings of the massacre were sent to all the Jewish communities and they were given arms to defend themselves. There was a little fighting, but the plot failed and the Jews were saved.

Children from the Jewish Sabbath class had painted many pictures of the story and hung them in the entrance hall of the synagogue. David, looking at some of the more gory paintings of Haman's death, ruefully remembered what the rabbi had said: "We must rejoice that the Jews were saved, but never rejoice that other people were killed."

During the evening service, the young people fidgeted impatiently, clutching greggers of many shapes and sizes. After the final blessing, officials with collecting boxes moved quickly round the synagogue.
    "What's the money for?" whispered Paul.
    "This year it's to be given to refugees from the earthquake in Yugoslavia," his father replied.

*Megillah*

59

Excitement grew when the rabbi held up a small scroll in a beautiful silver case. This was the **megillah**, or scroll of Esther. Carefully unrolling it, the rabbi prayed: "Blessed art Thou, O Lord our God, King of the Universe . . . who has given us a command concerning the reading of the megillah . . . ."

There was silence as the first two chapters were read. But when Haman's name was first mentioned in Chapter 3, all the children jumped to their feet, swinging their rattles and shouting and booing. Paul shuffled his feet loudly, sat down, and looked at the soles of his shoes. He'd chalked Haman's name on them while waiting for the service to begin. Now, he was delighted to see, none of the chalk-marks remained. After that, every time Haman's name was mentioned, the children booed, and every time Esther's name was mentioned, they cheered.

*Children rattling greggers*

When the story was finished, the rabbi read Psalm 22, which begins with a cry of despair: "My God, why hast Thou forsaken me?" As he continued reading, the message changed into one of hope. God would help the psalmist! Finally he gave the closing blessings: "Blessed art Thou, O Lord our God, King of the Universe, who dost plead our cause, judge all sins, and avenge any wrongs."

After the service Miriam rushed off to join her friends from the youth club. They quickly changed into colourful costumes. Some had brought lanterns. Miriam had her father's torch. Singing and dancing, they visited many Jewish houses, collecting money for the refugees.

"Today is Purim, tomorrow no more.

Give me a penny, I'll be gone from your door."

Many people also gave them cakes, sweets and soft drinks. By the end of the evening they were very tired, but their tiredness was soon forgotten when they realized they'd collected over fifty-seven pounds!

Paul couldn't wait to get to school next morning. It was the best day of the year. No lessons!

At Assembly, the top class read extracts from the Book of Esther in English and Hebrew. Then the younger ones went into another room to sing Purim songs, like this one:

I love the day of Purim, where all are gay and free,
I love the day of Purim, with gifts for you and me,
I love to go to the synagogue to hear the megillah read,
And cheer for dear old Mordecai and chop off Haman's
head.
With a gregg, gregg, gregg . . . gregg, gregg, gregg . . .
That's how Purim began.

Meanwhile, the Headmaster showed the older children two beautiful megillahs which he'd borrowed from the synagogue. He explained that the book wasn't a history book but a novel and, like a parable, it had a hidden meaning. God had saved

61

the Jews on many, many occasions when their enemies had tried to destroy them. And He always would.

Then Paul and his friends acted out the story in front of the whole school. He was Haman, and he'd had great fun making up. He had a big red nose and a long black curling moustache. He didn't mind a bit when everyone booed each time he appeared.

Purim is a time for giving presents. So before lunch each class visited another class-room, exchanging small gifts — sweets, a biro, a magazine. Paul was given a very useful notebook. His teacher explained that they should give presents to anyone in need. At school dinner they had **kreplach**, three-cornered dough pasties filled with meat and dropped into bowls of soup, followed by **Hamantashen** ("Haman's ears"!), three-cornered pasties filled with poppy seeds. The canteen staff, many of whom were not Jewish, had had great fun making them.

*Purim fancy-dress party*

In the afternoon, they had a school fair. All the parents were invited. Each class organized games and competitions. In Paul's class-room there was a lucky dip, and a blindfold game in which you had to pin the tail on Haman's horse! Paul's teacher showed some slides she'd taken of Purim carnivals in Israel. They showed beautifully decorated floats, folk concerts, people dancing, street mimes and firework displays.

Paul spent half an hour in his own class-room and then he was free to visit the other class-rooms with Gran and his mother. He was very skilful at throwing balls at little wooden figures of Haman and his ten sons. He knocked them all down twice and won a rubber shaped like a pineapple and a felt-tipped pen. Gran won two hankies for guessing correctly the number of dried peas in a gregger.

Finally the Headmaster announced that they'd collected over a hundred pounds for the children's hospital in Jerusalem.

# 11
# Passover:
# A Festival of Freedom

Mrs Singer smiled nervously at her visitors. They were girls and boys from a local comprehensive school who were studying Judaism for their O-level Religious Studies exam. They'd come to ask her questions about the Passover which was to be celebrated the following week.

"Who's going to ask the first question?"

"Why is it called Passover?" asked one of the girls.

"During the festival we remember how Moses led the Hebrews out of Egypt where they'd been slaves. Just before they left, the angel of death killed many Egyptian children but 'passed over' the houses of the Israelites. And so we call it Passover. Moses led the Hebrews to Mount Sinai. There God spoke to them. He'd chosen them to be a new nation, which would bear witness to Him and show Him at work in the world. He gave them the Law, which stressed both His love for them and the responsibility He laid upon them."

"How did they celebrate the feast in the time of Jesus?"

"Thousands of Jews came to Jerusalem from all over the known world. Every inn was full. Every house welcomed the pilgrims freely – although guests usually gave the skins of the sacrificed animals to their hosts. Tents were set up in every open space in and around the city. Many came to trade as well as to worship. Merchants sold animals for sacrifice, spices, wheat cakes, fish, wine, jewellery and souvenirs. Tailors mended torn coats and talliths, cobblers repaired shoes which had become worn during the journey.

"During the afternoon before Passover Eve there were three services at which the sacrifices were made. People who only managed to reach the Temple for the last service were accused of being lazy-bones! As darkness fell, the animals were cooked and eaten. No one went hungry because it was an honour to welcome a poor person or a stranger to share your meal."

The next question came from one of the boys.

"Can you tell me something about unleavened bread?"

"Well, the Israelites had a good meal before they fled from Egypt. But because they were in a hurry, they didn't have time to wait for the dough to rise before cooking it. Today we eat **matzoth**, or unleavened bread, to remind us of that part of the story. Matzoth contain no raising agent, and they are also perforated to stop them rising. In older times the perforations were often very decorative. One famous rabbi used animal and flower designs. In medieval Europe they used to have large communal ovens for baking the matzoth. In 1875 the first matzoth machine was invented in England. But rabbis still superintended the baking."

*Heaps of matzoth in a Jewish bakery around the turn of the century*

*Today matzoth are produced and packaged in factories, but the baking is still supervised by a rabbi.*

"I've heard people mention **chomets**," said a girl. "What are they?"

"All next week I'll be spring-cleaning the house in readiness for Passover – scrubbing, polishing, washing curtains. The day before the festival I'll carefully get rid of all the leavened bread and pastry in the house, for no crumbs must be left. But I'll put a little aside for the next day's breakfast, and I'll hide the chomets. These are large crumbs of leavened bread. When my husband comes home from the evening service at the synagogue he'll take a small bunch of goose feathers or willow twigs, and, with the children's help, search for these chomets. When he finds them, he'll sweep them into a wooden spoon and wrap it in a clean cloth. After breakfast next day, I'll add any left-overs and all the leavened bread will be burnt."

"You use special dishes and kitchenware for the festival, don't you?"

66

"Yes, we have separate sets of pans and dishes if we can afford them. These will never have been in contact with leaven. But if we can't afford a second set, we scald our everyday pans, cutlery and glassware in boiling water. The rabbis used to do this, using huge cauldrons of boiling water. Even today, in Mea Shearim, the religious district of Jerusalem, you can see them 'koshering' the dishes in the streets."

"How do you know what to do and say at the Passover meal?"

"The ceremony and the meal are both called the **Seder**. We have a book which tells us which special prayers to say. It's called the **Haggadah**, which means 'telling'. It also contains the questions the youngest boy traditionally asks about the meaning of the meal, and the answers he's given, together with psalms, stories, children's folk tales, riddles and songs. The meal and the ceremony last many hours and the stories and songs help the younger children keep awake – but we all enjoy them."

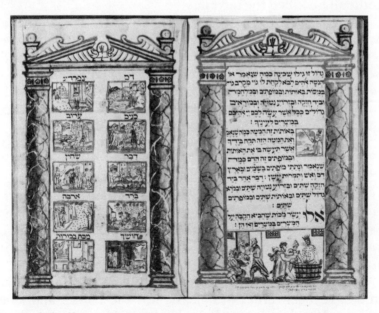

*Haggadah illustrating the story of the plagues of Egypt*

67

"Why do you celebrate something that happened over three thousand years ago?"

"For two reasons. We've often been imprisoned, persecuted and put to death. Yet God has helped us to survive. The Haggadah tells of the suffering of the Israelites and their deliverance from Egypt. But in our hearts we remember *all* the Jews who have suffered and *are* suffering. Many people add their own prayer to the Haggadah service. For example, American Jews sometimes pray for goodwill between people of all races, black and white. We sometimes pray for those who are hungry or homeless. One Haggadah has an extra prayer which says: 'Let us remember . . . the martyred Jews of all generations. Those who gave the world an eternal example of human courage, the heroes of **Masada**, the Jews who fought in the ghettos and in the concentration camps!' "

One of the boys said, "I've just read *Mila 18*. One passage in the book describes how the freedom fighters in the Warsaw ghetto celebrated the Passover although they knew they would all be killed the next day."

"It seems strange, perhaps, to you," Mrs Singer replied. "But many Jews in concentration camps celebrated the Seder, even when they only had a small crust of mouldy bread and a few drops of dirty rainwater instead of matzoth and wine. They thanked God for His help in the past and prayed that He would give the gift of freedom to men of all faiths in the future. You see, we pray not just for ourselves, but for others."

"You said there were two reasons for celebrating the feast today," a girl reminded her.

"Yes. The story of the Exodus symbolizes not only the right of all men to be free from slavery, but also their right to be free in their hearts and lives, free to choose between good and evil. Fear or greed or pride can make us slaves, can force us to do and say wrong things. Festivals like the Passover 'recharge our batteries' and give us strength to make the right decisions."

"One thing puzzles me," a girl remarked. "All the Egyptians can't have been cruel — at least, not the babies and small children. Yet the plagues hurt them too. How can you be so happy when many innocent people must have suffered and died before the Israelites were set free?"

"Many rabbis have asked this question. We are often told to grieve for the innocent and also to feel sorry for our enemies and forgive them. To help remember this at the Seder, a glass of wine is used when the story of the plagues is told. At the mention of each plague, we spill a little wine to show that our joy is tinged with sadness."

"We must go now, Mrs Singer," said one of the boys as they gathered their belongings. "Thanks for giving us so much help. Have a happy Passover next week."

The Passover meal was over. David lay in bed thinking about the Seder they'd just celebrated. He thought about his mother lighting the candles and saying the blessing over them, and about his father holding up the matzoth plate, covered with a lovely cloth, and saying: "This is the bread of affliction which our fathers ate in the land of Egypt. Let all who are hungry come and eat. Let all who are in need come and celebrate Passover with us."

*Passover plate with labels for the symbolic foods*

69

*At the Seder, the youngest male asks the four traditional questions. His father's answers remind the family of the first Passover celebration.*

David himself had helped fill the Passover plate. The roasted egg symbolized the Temple sacrifice, the bitter herbs symbolized all those who were oppressed, the parsley dipped in salt water represented all who were hungry. The haroseth, a mixture of nuts, fruit and spices, represented the mortar used by the Hebrew slaves and also the sweetness of God's love which makes slavery bearable. Finally, the lamb bone symbolized the lamb killed by the Israelites.

Four times his father had filled the wine cups, symbolizing God's four promises to free the Hebrews: "I shall take you unto me as a people."

Paul, the youngest male at the table, had asked the four questions about the Seder meal without faltering. He had learnt the words carefully at school. When he asked his father why he rested against a cushion, Mr Singer proudly replied: "I'm resting because I'm free."

David thought about the final prayer: "We have eaten our Passover meal as free men. Let us give thanks to the source of all life and freedom. May He who is most compassionate bless this house."

On his bedside table was a book about the Vietnamese refugees. Some of them described how they'd fled from their country, seeking freedom. They'd travelled in small boats, many of which had sunk; people had drowned. One chapter in the book was called "The Exodus". David prayed that God would help the refugees find freedom.

Soon it would be his bar-mitzvah. Then he would thank God that he was free to worship as he wished, free to be a Jew. As he fell asleep, David resolved that at the bar-mitzvah service he would promise to do all he could throughout his life to help others find freedom.

# 12
# A Death in the Family

Gran was dead. The children couldn't believe it. The rabbi found them huddled together round the kitchen table. Quietly he sat down.

"It's good to grieve for a little while," he said. "You loved your grandmother. Of course you'll miss her."

"Did she know she was dying?" asked Miriam.

"Yes. But she wasn't afraid, and she was able to say the prayer all Jews try to say at this time."

"What prayer?" said David.

"Understand, O Israel, the Lord our God is One. I acknowledge before Thee, my God, that my recovery and death are in Your hand. May it be Your will to heal me completely, but if I should die, may my death be an atonement for all the sins I have committed . . . in Your peace is complete joy, and happiness always at Your right hand."

"But God didn't make her better," sobbed Paul.

"No," the rabbi replied gently. "But Jews accept that death is a natural part of life. Your grandmother accepted God's will, and died peacefully, because she knew God had forgiven any wrongs she'd done. She would be close to Him, so she had nothing to fear."

David hesitated, then asked, "Rabbi, what *does* happen to us after we die?"

There was a pause. "Many people have tried to imagine exactly what it will be like. Some have tried to put their thoughts into words, using picture language, symbols and parables. For example, some have imagined two different

72

places – Heaven, where those who have been forgiven will live happily with God, and Hell, where those who haven't asked for forgiveness will live in pain, cut off from Him.

"Jews firmly believe in a life after death. We even call the cemetery **Bet Hahayyim**, 'House of Life'. But we believe we cannot know what it will be like. What we *do* know is that God is loving and merciful, and wants everyone to seek His forgiveness, and to find peace. Now, let us say together the short prayer Jews always say when they hear that someone has died."

Very quietly the children repeated, "Blessed are You, Lord our God, King of the Universe, the true Judge."

Later on, David and the rabbi went for a walk round the garden. "What will happen now?" David asked.

"Our synagogue has a group of voluntary helpers, the **Hevra Kadisha**, the Holy Brotherhood," the rabbi answered. "They'll make all the arrangements for your grandmother to be buried in the Jewish cemetery, and they will take care to ensure that all our traditional customs are followed."

"What are these customs?"

"Long ago some Jews had expensive and elaborate funerals. Poor people often felt ashamed because they couldn't do the same, so the rabbis decided that all funerals should be very simple. After all, everyone is equal before God.

"The body is dressed in a simple white garment of linen or wool. If the dead person is a man, his tallith is placed over his head and shoulders. The coffin is plain and made of wood."

"When will the funeral be?"

"As soon as possible. Probably tomorrow."

"My friend, Alan, lives next door. He's a Christian. When his father died last year, he was cremated."

"Yes. Some Christians ask to be buried, others to be cremated. Orthodox Jews always bury their dead. But some people are burned to death in accidents, or during times of persecution. Of course this will not matter to God. Nor will it make any difference if people of other faiths are cremated. All men can seek forgiveness – and find it."

73

They returned to the kitchen.

"Remember," said the rabbi, "we never leave a dead body alone. It's a mark of respect. Your parents will want to stay with your grandmother, quietly praying. So you and Miriam will have to make sure that Paul isn't lonely."

Mr Singer and David went to the funeral with the other male relatives and friends. They had both made a small tear in their jackets.

"This is called **Keriah**," said Mr Singer. "It's a very old custom – it means that we put the mark of sadness on our clothes." He also explained that it was customary for the women and children to stay at home.

The service was very simple and short. There were no flowers. Psalms and prayers were said: "O Lord, who is full of compassion . . . God of forgiveness . . . grant pardon to Elizabeth Singer, who has gone to her eternal home . . . shelter her for ever under the cover of Your wings and let her soul be bound up in the bond of eternal life . . . may she rest in peace."

Friends and relatives carried the coffin to the graveside. As it was lowered into the grave, the rabbi prayed, "May she come to her place in peace."

At home, Miriam and Paul sat quietly with their mother, while neighbours and friends prepared a light but nourishing meal. Mrs Singer explained to them what traditional customs must be followed.

"For the next seven days, a candle will burn continuously in our house. We won't prepare meals, cut our hair, wear leather shoes, or use make-up. We will sit on low stools instead of chairs, and we will put covers over all the mirrors. Friends will do everything that is necessary. Your father won't go to work and you won't go to school. Each day people will visit us, and we'll have a short service here. We'll say a special prayer called **Kaddish**."

"What does it say?" said Paul.

"Well, it isn't a sad prayer. We tell God we have faith in Him and in His justice: 'Glorified and sanctified be God's

74

great name throughout the world . . . may He create peace for us.' However unhappy we are, we know that He cares for us and that there is meaning and purpose in everyone's life."

"Will Dad go back to work after the seven days?" asked Paul.

"Yes, and you'll go back to school. But we won't wear new clothes, or go to parties or the cinema for another three weeks. And because Gran was Dad's mother, he won't do any of these things for a year. On the first anniversary of Gran's death, we'll light a twenty-four-hour candle here at home, your father will go to the synagogue to recite Kaddish, and we'll all visit the grave. Now, no more questions. Here are your father and David. Soon we'll be having something to eat."

JF - F

# THINGS TO DO, THINGS TO DISCUSS

Chapters 9–12

1 Organize a class discussion on freedom and free will.

2 Listen to a record of music for a Jewish service, or to recordings of Israeli folk-songs. If you have a record of *Fiddler on the Roof*, play the extracts that describe Jewish traditions and a Jewish wedding.

3 Plan a Purim concert for handicapped children or older people, making sure that everyone can join in the fun. Cassette tapes about Purim might give you some ideas.

4 Find out all you can about the Passover meal. Design your own Passover plate.

5 What do you believe about life after death? Try to express your thoughts in writing, music or painting.

# 13
# Shavuot:
# The Festival of Pentecost

"In three days' time we'll be celebrating the festival of **Shavuot**. Can you give me another name for it?" The rabbi looked round at the boys who'd come to bar-mitzvah class. "Reuben?"

"The Feast of Weeks – because it comes seven weeks after the second day of Passover."

"Or the feast of **Pentecost**," said James, "because it's fifty days after the first night of Passover."

"Good. David, why do we celebrate Shavuot?"

"Because we want to remember the most important event in our history when God gave the Torah to Moses on Mount Sinai. When Moses told the Israelites about the Ten Commandments, they all shouted, 'All that the Lord has spoken, we will do.' And at the synagogue service, like them, we promise to love and obey the Law."

"Yes! It's a very precious gift! Passover, when the Israelites were freed from slavery, is the 'beginning' festival. But this freedom meant very little to them until they had replaced the earthly rule of a cruel tyrant with the heavenly rule of a merciful and just God. So the Bible gives the festival a fourth name, **Atzeret**, or the 'concluding' festival. It's the same for every human being. We're all slaves because of the wrong and thoughtless things we so easily do and say – often with enjoyment! Only if we obey the Law, and love and serve God and other people, are we really free."

"Why do we decorate our homes and synagogues with leaves and flowers?" asked Simon.

"Because the Torah was given to Moses at the time of a harvest festival. We often use picture language when we describe the Torah. It's described as wine which brings joy, or oil which comforts our wounds, or water which cleanses and refreshes us and gives us life. Can you think of another image, Simon?"

"Mm . . . The Torah is the Tree of Life. That's why some Jews decorate their synagogues by putting growing trees on both sides of the Ark."

"We sometimes say that all other plants die, but the word of God lives for ever. Reuben, can you remember the verse in the Bible which tells us that?"

"Er . . . 'the grass withereth . . . the flower fadeth . . . but the word of our God lives for ever.'"

"And, David, can you remember a story to illustrate this?"

"A leaf wanted to escape from the branch of the tree. It wanted to be free to explore the world. One day a storm wind whirled it away into the sky. It had a wonderful view! But when the wind died down, the leaf fell to the ground and died."

"And the meaning?"

"Only if we stay close to the teaching of the Torah can we live good lives in this world, and continue to live with God after we die."

"Now, what do some Jewish men like to do on the night of Shavuot? James."

"My father will follow the old custom of spending the whole night in the synagogue reading the Torah and other religious books."

"I'm going to stay up with Dad this year," said David. He laughed. "Miriam says I'll go to sleep and not wake up till lunch-time!"

"And what will we do at the morning service?"

"First we'll recite some of the psalms of David, because we believe David was born and died on this day."

"And then, Simon?"

"We'll sing a prayer written in Aramaic nearly a thousand

78

years ago – the **Akdamut Milin**. We'll praise God and the Torah and remember the promise that all who study the Torah will find peace. The prayer ends with a description of the coming of the Messiah when everyone will find peace and happiness."

"David, can you quote any part of it?"

"I think so . . . .

> Could we with ink the ocean fill, were every blade of grass a quill,
> Were the world of parchment made, and every man a scribe by trade,
> To write the love of God above would drain the ocean dry,
> Nor would the scroll contain the whole, tho' stretched from sky to sky."

"On the second day we read the book of Ruth," said Reuben.

"What's that about?"

"Ruth was a Moabite princess and she didn't like worshipping cruel idols. She married into a family of Israelite refugees who'd fled from a famine in Judah. However, her husband and father-in-law soon died. Her mother-in-law, Naomi, decided to go home to Judah. She told Ruth to return to the comfort of her own parents' home. But Ruth had come to love God and the Torah and she insisted on going with Naomi. She said: 'Thy people shall be my people, and thy God my God.' Later, gleaning in the fields near Bethlehem, she attracted the attention of Boaz, a relative of Naomi's. She married him – and her great-grandson was King David!"

"Yes, Ruth loved the Torah, and at Shavuot we all tell God that we love the Torah too. Did you know," the rabbi continued, "that about a hundred and fifty years ago, Reform synagogues introduced a new custom at Shavuot? Many synagogues follow it now. Girls had begun to feel left out when the boys had their bar-mitzvah celebrations. And very

79

often, older boys felt they hadn't really understood the promises they'd made at thirteen. So the Reform rabbis began to hold a confirmation service for boys and girls of sixteen or seventeen years of age. After listening to readings from the Law the young people stand up and say, 'All that the Law has spoken we will do' – just like the Hebrews did at Mount Sinai over three thousand years ago. Now, it's time to go home."

"Shalom," said David. "I'm coming to the service with my uncle and aunt and my little cousin, Joshua. He's nearly five. Uncle says he wants to follow the old custom of bringing his son to the synagogue on Shavuot to listen to the Torah reading for the first time. Then at lunch he'll have his first Hebrew lesson. Mother's making some letters of the Hebrew alphabet out of pastry and dipping them in honey – that way, he's sure to enjoy his first lesson!"

At school, Miriam's friends asked her if she would be eating any special foods during Shavuot.

"Yes – we'll have two round loaves, decorated with a ladder to symbolize Moses going up and down Mount Sinai."

The Home Economics teacher overheard what Miriam said. "Why not bring some of your mother's recipes to class next week?" she suggested. "We'll make some of your festival dishes. I'll give you some money to buy the ingredients. Then we can be sure they're kosher!"

Here are some of the recipes they used:

## HOLISHKES (STUFFED CABBAGE) FOR SIMCHAT TORAH

12 large cabbage leaves
450 grams minced meat
50 grams rice
2 large onions, minced
25 grams chicken fat or margarine
½ teaspoon salt

2 tablespoons sugar
1 teaspoon lemon juice
3 tablespoons tomato purée
stock to cover

Wash the cabbage leaves, then pour boiling water over them to blanch them. Cut off the hard stalks. Mix together the meat, rice and one onion. Place some of the meat mixture on each leaf and roll up like a parcel. Melt the fat in a pan and fry the other onion. Add the cabbage rolls. Pour in enough stock to cover them, then add the salt, sugar, lemon juice and tomato purée. Cook very slowly for 3 hours. (To cook holishkes in the oven, put them in a casserole with a tightly fitting lid. Cook for 3 hours at Gas Mark 3 or 325° F (170° C).)


## DREIDEL CAKES (SPINNING-TOPS) FOR CHANUKAH

100 grams margarine
100 grams caster sugar
2 eggs
100 grams self-raising flour
1 level teaspoon baking-powder
grated rind of 1 lemon

Place all the ingredients in a bowl. Beat with a wooden spoon until smooth. Pour the mixture into a greased tin about 18 cm square. Bake on the middle shelf of the oven at Gas Mark 3 or 325° F (170° C) for 40–45 minutes. Cool on a wire tray and store overnight.

*Icing and decoration*
450 grams icing sugar, sieved
4 tablespoons water
1 tablespoon lemon juice
apricot jam, warmed and sieved
glacé cherries, angelica and sultanas
cocktail or lolly sticks

Cut the cake into 16 squares. Place these on a wire tray and brush the top and sides of each cake with apricot jam. Mix together the icing sugar, water and lemon juice, stirring well. Pour over the cakes, making sure all the sides are coated. Run a cocktail or lolly stick through the middle of each cake. Turn the cakes on their sides and decorate with strips of angelica forming the Hebrew letters nun, gimmel, heh and shin. Put a cherry at one end of each stick and a sultana at the other. Serve the cakes in paper cases.

nun     gimmel     heh     shin

## LOCHSHEN FOR PASSOVER

2 eggs
salt and pepper
oil

Beat the eggs and add the seasoning. Pour a little oil into a frying pan. When the oil is hot, pour in enough egg to cover the base of the pan in a thin layer. When cooked, turn over and cook the other side. Turn on to a flat plate. Repeat the process until the mixture is finished. Roll up each pancake and cut it into narrow strips (lochshen). Drop into boiling soup, cook for 2 minutes and serve.

## HAMANTASCHEN FOR PURIM

125 grams margarine
125 grams caster sugar
100 grams plain flour
100 grams self-raising flour } sieved together
1 egg yolk
melted honey
hundreds and thousands

Place the margarine, caster sugar, egg yolk and flour together in a bowl. Beat well with a wooden spoon to form a dough. Knead well on a lightly floured board and roll out thinly. Cut into rounds using a plain cutter about 7 cm in diameter (this amount of pastry should give you about 24 rounds). Put a teaspoonful of filling in the middle of each circle of pastry. Dampen the edges and draw them together to make triangular pyramids. Place well apart on a greased baking sheet. Bake on the top shelf of the oven at Gas Mark 7 or 425° F (220° C) for 20–25 minutes. Brush with melted honey and sprinkle with hundreds and thousands.

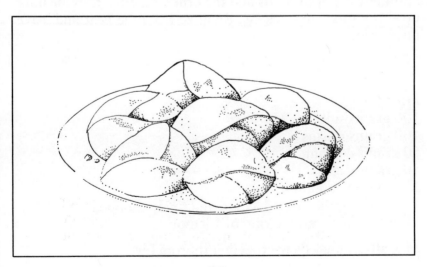

*Prune filling*
200 grams prunes (dried)
rind of 1 lemon and 1 orange
50 grams brown sugar

Soak the prunes overnight with the lemon and orange rinds and enough water to cover them. The following day, simmer the mixture gently until the liquid has evaporated. Remove the rind and the stones. Mince or finely chop the filling. (To use tinned prunes instead of dried ones, drain them, remove the stones and mix with some finely grated lemon or orange rind.)

*Poppy seed filling*
100 grams poppy seeds
150 ml milk
rind of 1 lemon, finely grated
50 grams sugar
25 grams margarine
25 grams sultanas
a little wine (optional)

Simmer the poppy seeds and the other ingredients in the milk until the mixture thickens. Remove from the heat and leave until cold.

*Fruit filling*
100 grams sultanas
100 grams raisins
50 grams currants
50 grams sugar
1 teaspoon cinnamon
1 cooking apple, peeled, cored and finely chopped
juice and finely grated rind of 1 lemon

Mix all the ingredients together thoroughly.

# CHEESECAKE FOR SHAVUOT

*Base*
50 grams margarine
25 grams caster sugar
75 grams plain flour, sieved

Grease a deep, loose-bottomed cake tin about 16 cm in diameter. Place the ingredients in a bowl and beat with a wooden spoon. Knead the dough lightly and press into the base of the tin.

*Filling*
100 grams margarine
100 grams caster sugar
2 eggs
450 grams curd cheese
25 grams self-raising flour
4 tablespoons cream or top of the milk
½ teaspoon vanilla sugar or vanilla essence
1 teaspoon lemon juice

Mix the ingredients in a bowl, beating with a wooden spoon until smooth. Pour over the base and smooth the top with a spoon dipped in milk. Bake on the middle shelf of the oven at Gas Mark 4 or 350° F (180° C) for 1¼–1½ hours, until set. Turn off the oven and leave until cold.

# 14
# David celebrates his Bar-mitzvah

David lay in bed looking up at the ceiling. It was very early, only six o'clock. Today was Shabbat, the first Shabbat after his thirteenth birthday. Today he celebrated his bar-mitzvah.

His eyes wandered to the wardrobe. On the top shelf, neatly folded in tissue paper, was a new man-size tallith. It was still a little large for him, but his grandmother had bought it for him just before she died.

On the dressing-table lay his tefillin, a present from his parents. From today he'd be treated as an adult Jew. He'd wear tefillin each weekday when saying morning prayers, whether in the synagogue or at home. But, as this was Shabbat, he wouldn't wear them at the service. Surrounded by examples of God's love and care, he wouldn't need them to help him concentrate on his prayers.

An adult! Increasingly now, he'd be responsible before God for his own actions; anything he did wrong would be a sin before God. He could be called up to read the Torah in the synagogue, and he could be a member of the **minyan**, the minimum ten males without whom a synagogue service couldn't take place.

Silently, David repeated the blessings he was to recite in the synagogue later in the morning – and the passage he'd memorized from the Prophets. He was glad he could easily get his tongue round the Hebrew words, and after attending bar-mitzvah class for two years, he'd mastered the old, simple melodies used by the cantors. He smiled with relief – thank goodness he'd done well in the bar-mitzvah examinations.

He thought about the party he would have the next day. He knew there'd be lots of presents from his family and friends.

*Jewish family celebrating a bar-mitzvah at the Western Wall*

He'd asked that many of his presents should take the form of money. He wanted to save up for a trip to Israel. Each year the synagogue organized a visit for young people aged between fifteen and eighteen. He so much wanted to see Jerusalem.

He was very glad it wasn't going to be a very grand party. As it was, it would be hard enough to make a speech in front of so many people. He'd been worrying about it for weeks. Then, yesterday, his mother had solved his problem. After meeting the O-level class, she'd bought a copy of *Mila 18*. It was difficult for him to read it all, but she'd shown him the passage about Stephan's bar-mitzvah in occupied Poland in 1943. Stephan had understood that it was easy to promise to be a faithful Jew when things were going well – but in Warsaw, at that time, he knew it would need great courage and commitment to stand firm for his faith. David had decided to begin his speech by reading out this passage. Then he'd tell the rabbi, his parents and his friends that it had helped him to understand that he must not take his religion lightly. He'd go on learning more and more about his faith, so that if he should ever be mocked or persecuted he'd have the courage to remain faithful to God and the Torah.

There were many members of David's family and many friends at the synagogue.

After the morning prayers, the congregation stood as the cantor took the **Sefer Torah** containing the Five Books of Moses from the Ark, saying, "Blessed is He who gave the law to His people, Israel."

David, his father and uncle, and other male members of his family were called up to the bimah. They stood beside the rabbi as he read portions of the Law. David himself read the last lesson from Deuteronomy, the portion chosen for that Shabbat. He followed the Hebrew text, carefully tracing the words from right to left with the silver yad given to him by the cantor. When he had finished, the scroll was held up so that all could see it, then returned to the Ark. Next, David chanted the reading from the Prophets, the Haftarah.

Everyone except David and the rabbi left the bimah. The rabbi shook David's hand and gave him a copy of the Siddur, the service book, bound in black leather. He told David how much his family contributed to the life of the synagogue. He added that David, too, was an active member of the synagogue and that he'd been a good student. He looked forward to helping David understand more about what it meant to be a Jew, and to enjoy being a Jew.

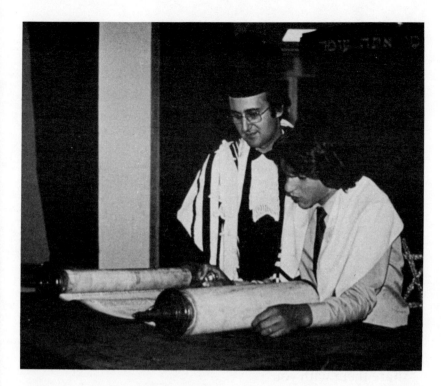

*"A son of the commandment"*

"And I would like you to memorize this verse from the prophet Micah," said the rabbi.

> "Now the Lord has told us what is good.
> What He requires of us is this: to do what is just,
> to show constant love, and to live in humble
> fellowship with our God."

He put his hand on David's shoulder.

> "The Lord bless you and keep you,
> The Lord make His face to shine upon
> you and give you peace."

89

# THINGS TO DO, THINGS TO DISCUSS

Chapters 13 and 14

1 Read some Jewish prayers. What do they tell you of Jewish beliefs about God?

2 Try out some Jewish recipes at home or at school. Invite members of staff, parents and friends to a small buffet meal and ask for donations to help a local Jewish charity, or a charity advertised in the *Jewish Chronicle*.

3 Prepare an Assembly on an aspect of Judaism that may help other people in the school to understand what it means to be a Jew.

4 When celebrating your bar-mitzvah, or a similar ceremony, what promises would you like to make and why?

5 Ask your teacher to find a book of Jewish stories and to share them with you.

# Resources/Useful Addresses

A wealth of resource material relating to the Jewish faith is now available. The following organizations offer a wide variety of books, pamphlets, audio-visual programmes, records, games, posters, etc. Some also sell ceremonial and religious items used in Jewish worship, and others arrange courses for Jewish and non-Jewish teachers and pupils. When writing off for catalogues or other information, please remember to enclose a stamped, addressed envelope for the reply.

The Education Officer
Board of Deputies of British Jews
Woburn House
Upper Woburn Place
London WC1H 0EP

Jewish Education Bureau
8 Westcombe Avenue
Leeds LS8 2BS

The Jewish National Fund Publishing Co.
Youth and Education Department
Harold Poster House
Kingsbury Circle
London NW9 9SP

## OTHER USEFUL ADDRESSES

The Jewish Bookshop
Woburn House
Upper Woburn Place
London WC1H 0EP

The Bookshop stocks a great number of books on all aspects of Jewish culture, religion and history, and can also provide details of mail order services, records, tapes, catalogues, etc.

JF - G

Local teachers' centres can often advise teachers and pupils on questions about Judaism. Specific requests may also be sent to the author by writing to:

The Information Officer
The SHAP Working Party on World Religions in Education
City of Liverpool College of Higher Education
Liverpool Road
Prescot L34 1NP

## BOOK LIST

*All About Jewish Holidays and Customs*, Morris Epstein. Ktav.
*The Bar Mitzvah Book*, Moira Paterson (ed.). W. H. Allen.
*The Hanukkah Book*, Mae S. Rockland. Schocken.
*The Jewish Festivals*, H. Schauss. Schocken.
*Mila 18*, Leon Uris. Corgi.
*Passover, The Family, Marriage, The Synagogue, Sukkot* and other titles in the Popular Judaica series, R. Posner (ed.). Keter Publications.
*When a Jew Celebrates*, Harry Gersh. Behrman House.
*When a Jew Prays*, Seymour Rossel. Behrman House.

Stories can bring many new insights into a study of the Jewish family. A number of collections of appropriate stories, together with biographies and autobiographies, have appeared in print. Many are listed on pages 44–56 of *World Religions: a Handbook for Teachers*, edited by W. Owen Cole and published by Community Relations. This book is available from the Commission for Racial Equality, Elliot House, 10–12 Allington Street, London SW1E 5EH.

92

# Glossary

*Note: there are various ways of spelling some Jewish words. Chanukah, for example, may appear as Hanukah or Hanukkah, and Succoth as Sukkot.*

**Akdamut Milin**  a prayer recited during the service for the festival of Shavuot. It ends with a description of the coming of the Messiah.

**Apocrypha**  a collection of scriptures not included in the Christian canon or in the main collection of Jewish scriptures, but often read by both Christians and Jews. It includes the story of the Maccabees.

**Ark of the Covenant**  an alcove, cupboard or box on the wall of a synagogue, facing Jerusalem. The Ark contains the scrolls of the Law, which are used at services.

**Aron Hakodesh**  the Holy Ark. Another name for the Ark of the Covenant.

**Atzeret**  the "concluding" festival. Another name for the festival of Shavuot.

**bar-mitzvah**  literally, "the son of the commandment". A Jewish boy becomes bar-mitzvah and assumes responsibility before God for his actions when he reaches the age of thirteen. He can then fulfil religious duties, e.g. be counted as a member of the minyan. Usually the event is celebrated in the morning service on the Sabbath after the boy's thirteenth birthday, and by a party.

93

| B.C.E. and C.E. | the Jews have a special system of dating. Year 1 in the Jewish calender (the date Jews give to the creation of the world) corresponds to the Christian year 3760 B.C. This makes the Christian year A.D. 1982 the Jewish Year 5742, for example. However, Jews also find it practical to adopt a second system, almost identical to the Christian one. The only differences are that B.C.E. (before the Common Era) and C.E. (Common Era) are used instead of B.C. (before Christ) and A.D. (anno domini). To the Jews, therefore, the Christian year 1982 – A.D. 1982 – is both 5742 and 1982 C.E. |
| Bet Hahayyim | the House of Life. The Jewish name for a cemetery. |
| bimah | the platform either immediately in front of the Ark or in the centre of the synagogue from which the scrolls of the Law are read at public services. |
| cantor | the leader of the singing and chanting in synagogue services. |
| capel | a small skull-cap worn by many Jewish men and boys as a sign of respect to God. |
| Chanukah | literally, "dedication". Often known as the Feast of Light, this festival celebrates the rededication of the Temple by the Maccabees and is a symbol of freedom from oppression. |
| Chanukah gelt | coins given to children as gifts at Chanukah. |
| Chanukiah | the eight-branched candlestick which is used during the eight days of Chanukah. One candle is lit on the first day, two on the second, and so on. |
| chomets | foods containing leaven. For example, the small pieces of leavened bread hidden on the day before the feast of Passover. When |

94

|   |   |
|---|---|
| | found, they are ceremonially burnt. |
| **chuppah** | the wedding canopy beneath which the bride and groom exchange their marriage vows. It serves as a symbol of the home they are going to build. |
| **Deuteronomy** | the Book of the Law. The fifth book of the Torah and of the Old Testament. |
| **dreidel** | a four-sided spinning-top. The four Hebrew letters written on the sides represent the phrase Nes Gadol Haya Sham ("A great miracle happened here"). |
| **etrog** | a citron. Together with a palm branch (lulav), a myrtle branch and a willow leaf, this citrus fruit makes up the ceremonial cluster used in the celebration of the festival of Succoth. |
| **Exodus** | the departure of the Israelites (led by Moses) from slavery in Egypt in search of the Promised Land. Exodus is also the name of one of the books of the Torah and of the Old Testament. |
| **Genesis** | the beginning. The first book of the Torah and of the Old Testament. |
| **Haggadah** | literally, "narration". A book read at the Passover meal which describes the story of the Exodus and explains the symbols and rituals of the Seder service. |
| **hallot** | (singular, **hallah**) freshly baked braided loaves used at Sabbath and festival meals. |
| **Hamantaschen** | small three-corned pasties eaten at Purim. |
| **Havdalah** | literally, "separation". This service, performed in the home as well as in the synagogue, marks the end of the Sabbath. |
| **Hevra Kadisha** | the Holy Brotherhood. A group of voluntary helpers attached to a synagogue who help with funeral arrangements. |

95

| | |
|---|---|
| **Holy of Holies** | the inner sanctuary of the Temple which stood in Jerusalem. |
| **Kaddish** | a prayer in praise of God used in synagogue services. In one form, it is recited by mourners during the year following the death of a relative and on the anniversary of the death. |
| **Keriah** | literally, "rending". The garment of the mourner is torn as a sign of mourning. |
| **keter** | the crown, often made of silver, which decorates the Torah scrolls. |
| **ketubah** | the religious marriage certificate which describes the nuptial obligations of husbands and wives to each other. |
| **kiddush** | literally, "sanctification". The blessing in praise of God which is chanted over a cup of wine on Sabbaths and festivals, signifying that these are holy days. |
| **Kol Nidre** | literally, "all vows". The opening prayer of the service on the eve of Yom Kippur. |
| **kosher** | food that is ritually acceptable in accordance with Jewish religious practice. |
| **kreplach** | small pasties eaten with soup at the festival of Purim. |
| **latkes** | potato pancakes eaten during the festival of Chanukah. |
| **lulav** | palm branch (*see* etrog). |
| **Maccabees** | the leaders of a successful revolt by the Jews against their Graeco-Syrian oppressors. The revolt is commemorated at the festival of Chanukah. |
| **Masada** | a bleak hill-top fortress overlooking the Dead Sea which has become a symbol to all Jews fighting for their liberty. In 73 C.E. a small group of Jews made a last stand here against the Romans, who had conquered |

Jerusalem and destroyed the Temple. They chose to die by their own hands rather than be captured by the Romans.

**matzoth** (singular, **matzah**) unleavened bread eaten at Passover time to remind Jews of the "bread of affliction" eaten in haste as the Israelites prepared to leave Egypt under the leadership of Moses.

**megillah** literally, "a scroll". In the Hebrew Bible there are five books called megillot (plural): Ecclesiastes, Esther, the Song of Songs, Ruth and Lamentations.

**menorah** a seven-branched candlestick found in synagogues and Jewish houses, and once used in the Temple at Jerusalem.

**Messiah** literally, "one anointed with holy oil". A leader who will come to bring a time of peace and freedom to Israel.

**mezuzah** a small container placed on the right-hand doorposts of Jewish houses. It contains passages from the Hebrew Bible and reminds Jews to obey God both inside and outside their homes.

**minyan** literally, "number". A minyan or quorum of ten males over thirteen years of age is required before a public act of worship can take place.

**Neilah prayer** the prayer recited at the final service on Yom Kippur.

**Ner Tamid** literally, "Eternal Light". In every synagogue a light is kept burning over the Ark in memory of the light which burned in the Temple at Jerusalem, a symbol of God's presence there.

**Orthodox and Reform Judaism** Orthodox Jews adhere strictly to the written law of Moses and the oral law of the rabbis. Reform, Liberal and Conservative

97

Jewish movements, although firmly rooted in Biblical tradition, accept in varying degrees changes and innovations in ritual, custom and Biblical interpretation. For example, according to Orthodox Judaism, a man must walk, not drive, to the synagogue on the Sabbath. According to Reform Judaism, however, he may drive there if the nearest synagogue is many miles from his home (as often happens in Britain, for example).

**Parochet** the veil found in some synagogues which screens the Ark from the congregation.

**Passover** the feast commemorating the Exodus from Egypt. Also known as Pesach, it is one of three harvest festivals celebrated by Jews.

**Pentateuch** the Five Books of Moses: Genesis, Exodus, Leviticus, Numbers and Deuteronomy. Also known as the Sefer Torah. *See also* Torah.

**Pentecost** *see* Shavuot.

**Pesach** *see* Passover.

**the Prophets** the name given to a collection of books in the Hebrew Bible. It contains books other than the so-called prophetic books in the Christian Old Testament.

**Psalms** a book of chants and songs found in the Writings which are often recited at synagogue services.

**Purim** literally, "lots". This festival reminds Jews of the story of deliverance from evil recounted in the Book of Esther.

**rabbi** literally, "master". The title of teachers and leaders in Jewish communities.

**Rosh Hashanah** the New Year festival, celebrated in the autumn. At Rosh Hashanah the shofar is blown in the synagogue to call the congregation to repentance.

**Sabbath** Shabbat, or Saturday. The seventh day of the week, when God rested after creating the world (Genesis, Chapter 2). The Sabbath is celebrated from sunset on Friday to sunset on Saturday. It is a day of rest and fellowship.

**Seder** literally, "order of service". The name given to the ritual meal held in all Jewish homes on the first night of Passover.

**Sefer Torah** *see* Pentateuch.

**shamash** literally, "one who serves". The shamash helps in the administration of the synagogue and the community. This is also the name given to the "servant" candle from which the other candles on a Chanukiah are lit.

**Shavuot** literally, "weeks". Also known as Pentecost, it is one of the three harvest festivals celebrated by Jews, coming fifty days (seven weeks) after the second day of Passover.

**Schechita** the name given to the way in which animals are killed in the Jewish tradition.

**Shema** abbreviation for the Hebrew prayer Shema Israel ("Hear, O Israel, the Lord our God, the Lord is One").

**shofar** the horn of a kosher animal other than a cow – usually a ram – blown just before and during the New Year (Rosh Hashanah) services to remind people of their need to seek forgiveness for wrong thoughts and actions.

**Simchat Torah** literally, "rejoicing in the Law". A festival immediately following the feast of Tabernacles (Succoth), marking the ending and

99

| | beginning of the annual cycle of the reading of the Torah. |
|---|---|
| Siddur | the order of service, compiled over many centuries, which comprises the Jews' prayer book. |
| sofer | a scribe who writes out the Jewish scriptures by hand. |
| Succoth | the festival of Booths or Tabernacles. A succah (singular) is erected each year in Jewish homes and synagogues, and meals are eaten there whenever possible during the eight days of the festival. The frail structure of the succah symbolizes the dwellings erected by the Jews as they wandered in the wilderness after the Exodus. |
| Tabernacles | *see* Succoth. |
| tallith | the prayer shawl worn by males during prayer at home and in the synagogue. |
| Talmud | the books of Jewish law compiled by the rabbis in the post-Biblical period. |
| Taschlich | a ceremony practised at the festival of Rosh Hashanah. |
| tefillin | phylacteries. These are small boxes which a Jewish male straps to his head and arm while praying (except on Sabbaths and festivals). |
| Temple | the Temple at Jerusalem was originally built by Solomon in 960 B.C.E. Destroyed in 586 B.C.E. and rebuilt in 515 B.C.E., it was restored by Herod in about 20 B.C.E. The Temple was finally destroyed by the Romans in 70 C.E. |
| Torah | the Five Books of Moses, more correctly referred to as the Sefer Torah. The name can be used to mean all Jewish learning and culture, both biblical and rabbinic. |
| the Writings | a collection of books read by Jews at |

100

|              | services and at home which includes the Psalms and, together with the Prophets, is part of the Hebrew Bible. |
|--------------|----------------------------------------------------------------------------------------------------------------|
| yad          | a pointer with a hand at one end, used when reading the Torah scrolls. |
| yarmulka     | a small skull-cap (*see* capel). |
| Yizkor prayer | prayer recited by mourners on Yom Kippur and at the festivals of Succoth, Passover and Shavuot. |
| Yom Kippur   | the Day of Atonement, coming ten days after the beginning of the Jewish year. Jews fast for twenty-five hours as they seek and acknowledge God's forgiveness. |
| Zmirot       | traditional songs sung, for example, at the Festival of Passover. |